Feedback on *Dear Mallory*

Although all of the letters, both from her mother and from those who knew her, or knew *of* her, were tremendously moving, for me the most powerful letter in this book was the suicide note written by 18 year-old Mallory.

Obviously this book is not only a tribute to a much loved teenager, but an amazing though profoundly sad testimony to how far-reaching and deeply the tragedy of suicide impacts those left behind.

As the Director of TEEN LINE and a strong proponent of teen suicide prevention, I commend Lisa Richards for putting together such a powerful book. Anyone who takes the time to read these letters will be affected by the awful loss of an obviously talented young woman. I hope that any young person contemplating taking their own life will realize that doing so leaves a vacuum that no one else can fill.

Elaine Leader, Ph.D., CGP, FAGPA
Executive Director, TEEN LINE
Cedars-Sinai Medical Center

This heartfelt compilation of notes and letters starts with the suicide note of 18 year-old Mallory to her mother, and is followed by a multitude of letters to Mallory, written by her mother and many others who were profoundly touched by her loss. These letters not only share the painful feelings of loss, memories, and the questions of "why" so common after a suicide, but they also share gratitude and each writer's efforts to make Mallory's loss meaningful to them. These letters are poignantly personal, yet they speak to the universal experience of anyone who has been touched by suicide loss.

Nina J. Gutin, Ph.D
Co-Chair, Clinician-Survivors Task Force,
American Association of Suicidology;
Survivors After Suicide Program,
Didi Hirsch Mental Health Services
Los Angeles, CA

Dear Mallory

Letters to a Teenage Girl Who Killed Herself

Lisa Richards would like to thank the Anais Nin Trust for permission to quote from Anais Nin, ©The Anais Nin Trust. All Rights Reserved.

For Information:

New Middle Press Torrance
25202 Crenshaw Blvd. #200
Torrance, California 90505

Telephone Number: (866) 693-0443
www.newmiddlepress.com

For Mallory Erin Richards
In Loving Memory

May her precious life and tragic death help guide us toward
creating a wiser and more compassionate world for all.

Acknowledgements

I am grateful to many. The contributors to this book shared touching memories of my daughter, and struggled through their pain to address the unthinkable. Rita and Harold Stearn, along with Ken and Alyson Sann have shown me the ongoing love and devotion of family. Dear family friends Mali and Brian Erb, Erika Schlarmann and Mary Simun (all of whom are referenced in my letters to my daughter) have created for me a fortress of love. Raymond Scurfield, Ph.D., Danielle Lew, Laura Israel, L.C.S.W. and many others have extended themselves to me with continued support and friendship. The Compassionate Friends, especially Mort Schrag, have unflinchingly held out their mighty arm of courage and wisdom. So too has the Survivors After Suicide family helped me tremendously, especially Carol Chasin, MFT, Mary Gayman, Marilyn Nobori, and Rick Mogul. Cynthia Rubin-Brown, Psy.D., Veronica Abney, Ph.D., Charles Grob, M.D., Michele Berk, Ph.D. and others have born witness to the horrors of losing a child to suicide. Michael Baranov provided legal assistance for this manuscript. Bryan Ngo embraced this project with interest and helpfulness. Eric Loeb gave enthusiastic early manuscript assistance, as well as friendship and moral support well above and beyond the call of duty.

And, to my clients, who, for over twenty-five years have both trusted me, and taught me the power of the human spirit to persevere, and to learn from adversity, *Thank You.*

~~Lisa Richards

Dear Mallory

Letters to a Teenage Girl
Who Killed Herself

Compiled by Lisa Richards, L.C.S.W.

By Friends and Loved Ones of Mallory Erin Richards

About Lisa Richards

Lisa Richards, L.C.S.W. received her Masters degree in Social Work from the University of Southern California in 1983, and is a Board Certified Diplomat in Clinical Social Work. She sees clients in Torrance and Santa Monica, California. Lisa is also a clinical consultant to the Southern California business community, and she provides critical incident stress debriefing for aviation disaster and other catastrophic events.

Lisa's work has appeared in *Interface: Psychiatry and Medicine* (Del Amo Hospital) and *Clinical Social Work Journal.* She has been an invited guest speaker at numerous conferences.

Her daughter Mallory was her only child.

Contents

Foreword

Some 34,000 people die by suicide every year in the United States, which means that every 15 minutes, there are parents, brothers, sisters and countless others left suddenly behind. I have devoted my professional life to preventing this tragedy, so that families will not have to struggle with how to carry on following a suicide loss. Lisa Richards has also worked as a grief counselor for over twenty years, but she is forced now to find a way to console herself after her eighteen year-old daughter dies by suicide. A parent's worst nightmare is to bury their child.

I stand in awe of Lisa Richards' courage to passionately and intimately share with us her loss, refusing to be silenced by her daughter Mallory's suicide. I know from writing a memoir about my mother's suicide, the challenge and the unbearable pain of finding words to convey the yearning, the enormous loss and the desire to find a way to connect to someone who is absent. When reading Lisa's words, I vacillated between tears and admiration. She shares her sorrow about her daughter's irreversible act. Lisa will never be a grandmother. She brings fresh flowers to Mallory's crypt each week and sobs. To mark Mallory's nineteenth birthday, she eats vegan cupcakes and drops stones (symbolizing the heaviness of grief) into a basket, in exchange for a small painted ceramic heart, as she says aloud what she is grateful for, about Mallory's life. And she shares with us what have now become the heartbreaking words that Mallory would say when she was very small, before leaving Lisa, "Miss you need you love you want you."

Lisa draws us into her agony as she tries to figure out what signs she might have missed, including Mallory's "dangerous thinking patterns" that Lisa only later discovers hidden in Mallory's journals after her death. She is confused about why Mallory would have hidden her suffering in the weeks before she died. Lisa struggles to reconcile both her pride in who her daughter was, and her anticipated growth, with Mallory's suicide and jettisoned future. On Lisa's healing journey, she shows us that love lasts longer than death. Even as she aches to be present with her daughter in the living moments of intimacy, she insists that Mallory is "... the daughter I chose to love and adore." One is reminded of William Merwin's words, "Your absence has gone through me/Like thread through a needle. Everything I do is stitched with its color."

Although Lisa's strength and resilience are unquestionably tested, she shows us the endurance of the human spirit. With Lisa's testament of her love for Mallory, she offers hope to those who struggle to heal from bewildering loss. John O'Donohue comforts the family and friends of a suicide, "As you huddle around the torn silence, /Each by this lonely deed

exiled /To a solitary confinement of soul/ May some small glow from what has been lost/ Return like the kindness of candlelight."
You will feel gratitude to Lisa for taking us on a journey that offers consolation and a candlelight out of the darkness of grief.

Nancy Rappaport, M.D., Assistant Professor of Psychiatry, Harvard Medical School,
Author of *In Her Wake: A Child Psychiatrist Explores the Mystery of Her Mother's Suicide*

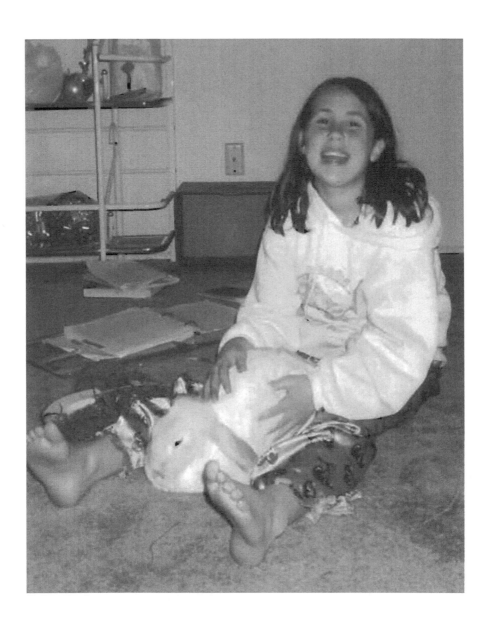

4

DEAR MOM,

  i LOVE you SO MUCH. I AM SO SORRY. i HAVE STALLED AND
HAVE waited to write this letter because i KNOW that
there is Nothing i could say to make this okay.

but i KNOW that you'll want to understand why this Happened.
i'll do My best to explain.

Honestly, i'VE been feeling totally overwhelmed with Life.
I Feel like Living Has become A series of <u>events</u> and
<u>emotions</u> And <u>tasks</u>, And it's too MUCH FOR ME.

i get stuck iN My HEAd aLot. i'M thinking And feeling all
the time. it's A struggle for ME. please understand that
this decision is Not impulsive. i AM not choosing to end My
Life because of Any situation at Hand. i simply Feel worn
out — depleted.

And <u>yes</u>. there are so many things that make Me Happy.
My RELationSHiP with you is At the top of the List.
you ARE extraordinary.
ultimately, the PAiN i feel takes over every time.
i've used coPing skills — but i Must be Missing something.
because Life shouldn't just be something to cope with.

i HOPE you KNOW How MUCH i LovE and care about you.
i KNow that you do.

you are always My favorite.
i Miss you already.
      ♡LOVE,
        MalloRY

Introduction

My eighteen year-old daughter Mallory has been, and always will be my greatest blessing. She was a playful, uninhibited little girl with a wonderful sense of humor, and she drank in life with a colossal thirst for whatever it offered her. Happy and resilient, as well as aware and expressive of her feelings from a young age, she gave me great hope that she would successfully navigate her way through life's challenges, whatever they might be, and build a life of her own design.

My daughter has made me laugh and cry. In her presence, as well as simply reflecting upon her presence in the world, I have felt boundless gratitude for both my motherhood and my life. My daughter has taught me what it means to love someone deeply, and without conditions. In her better moments, she often looked upon the world as a precious gift as well as a constant teacher of lessons that need to be learned. And she spent much of her youth doing two things she felt passionately about— entertaining people as a young actor in community theater, through summer drama camps for children and teens, and showing her generous compassion to others. She traveled as a Student Ambassador to Australia, impressed many adults with a wisdom beyond her years, and stood often as a source of love and inspiration to those who knew her. In middle school, she volunteered at a rabbit rescue organization. And, years later, at age seventeen, while she studied at Santa Monica College, she began to feed the homeless in Santa Monica every Saturday morning. To those who knew her, Mallory continuously unveiled in a myriad of ways her interest in the world becoming a more loving (read: less ego-driven) place.

In August 2010, just two weeks after her eighteenth birthday, Mallory and I visited several Northern California colleges that she had wanted to see, months after announcing her interest in pursuing a career in clinical social work. She loved the "nature hippie vibe" that she experienced at UC Santa Cruz, from where she said she wanted to get her undergraduate degree in Psychology before applying to social work schools. So upon returning from our trip, she began to line up her classes at Santa Monica College, to support her transfer goals. In October 2010, she was accepted into SMC's honor society, through which she sought out other opportunities to meet like-minded friends and to volunteer.

But my daughter is dead, now, a suicide.

One afternoon in January, 2011, five months after her eighteenth birthday, and that trip we took up north, Mallory killed herself at home, while I worked at my Santa Monica office. And my daughter's meticulously planned death not only stunned those who knew her, doctors and therapists included, but it also left a community of friends, loved ones and teachers grappling for understanding. For me, it was the absolute near-destruction of my soul.

My daughter left her diaries in plain view for me to find after she killed herself. Her more recent entries revealed that she had hidden with an actor's propensity for masquerade the return approximately five weeks before her death, of acute suicidal depression and anxiety, which had immobilized her in 2007 after she started high school. Back then, after she made three serious suicide attempts and repeatedly lied to me and her therapists about her safety, I boarded a plane with my daughter and enrolled her in an out-of-state therapeutic boarding school to try and save her life. She would spend the better part of the next two and a half years in such schools, (with me flying back and forth for visits and family therapy, and her coming home for passes) until she graduated from a year-round school in August 2009, and returned home to Southern California for good. Mallory's therapists and doctors were encouraged by her progress in intensive residential treatment, and cautiously optimistic about her prospects for a bright future.

Mallory and I moved to a new community to help give her a fresh start. She began outpatient therapy and was evaluated as needed by a psychiatrist. Both to her treatment providers and to me, my daughter seemed to be doing well, navigating her way through the big and small challenges of teenage life.

In the weeks before she killed herself, Mallory attended several holiday parties and get-togethers with friends, and she asked me to volunteer with her at a large Thanksgiving Day event in Santa Monica, for the homeless and underprivileged. She watched her friends and classmates perform in a school play one Sunday; on other days, she shopped for holiday gifts for her loved ones, watched movies and visited with a close friend, and walked arm-in-arm with me in mid-December one afternoon and evening along the cobblestone paths of a popular outdoor shopping mall where we ate, talked and window shopped. Her mood did indeed appear blunted at times during those weeks before her death, and there were, looking back, several instances of what were for her, in my experience, uncharacteristic instances of quiet belligerence that seemed out of proportion to anything going on between us at the time. But my few efforts to ask about these moments were met with, "Come on, Mom. This is just what teenagers and their parents go through sometimes. I talk to you more than most teenagers talk with their parents." Well, she was right—teenagers and their parents can indeed go through challenging times, and especially since she had received intensive treatment, she *had* generally seemed open with me about the important things that were on her mind. But she was also defending against a deeper truth when she spoke those words, because there were embryonic sensations brewing in me, that there might be a problem for my daughter. Her dismissive replies the several times I asked her what was going on, coupled with how well she had seemed to be doing since her return home almost one and a half years earlier resulted in me giving Mallory the benefit of the doubt. *It must be me*, I said to myself. *Maybe she's right, that I'm overreacting.*

And then she killed herself.

If I—or anyone—had known the dark contents of her more recent journal entries, or if she had asked someone—anyone—for help, my daughter might well be alive today. But the same talent for acting which had brought Mallory years of unbridled joy, mostly on the stage of the Redondo Beach Playhouse, was now used to conceal from all who knew and loved her, her devastating plan to end her life in the face of what she must have come to believe were insurmountable obstacles to living. I missed the clues she casually dropped, and she hid her dangerous thinking patterns beneath a calm exterior.

The journals my daughter kept from the time of her return home in 2009 told the story of a sensitive young girl trying desperately to fit into a world that all too often felt harsh and unyielding to her. It was a story of looking for acceptance in dangerous places, of deep episodic loneliness and self-doubt, and of opening her heart at times to people who she would experience as not treating her with the same loving-kindness she so routinely showed to others. Once Mallory's suicidal depression returned in full force, just after Thanksgiving 2010 (according to her journal entries), in spite of her show of teenage normalcy over the next five weeks, she had already begun her quiet, permanent detachment from this world.

My eighteen year-old daughter's remains now lie inside a powder blue casket entombed in a wall crypt at the cemetery. Her lifeless hands hold notes written to her by a young family member, her twelve year-old cousin Alyson, and two close friends who eulogized her before a crowd of almost two hundred stunned mourners on the Sunday following her death.

I was too grief-stricken at the time of her memorial service and burial to write a letter to my daughter; it was all I could do in those early days after her death, to put together, with the help of friends and family a memorial service that wouldn't be desecrated by my own shock and anguish. But fifteen days after Mallory died, I began speaking quietly to her, in the privacy of the home we once shared; and I knew, then, that I had to start writing to her, even though it would be an admittedly one-sided conversation. For the rest of my life.

In the months since my daughter died, I have had the opportunity to reconnect with some of her friends and mentors from years ago, as well as learning about and meeting people she befriended more recently in school, and in her volunteer work feeding the homeless. I also began to exchange correspondence with one mother and several donor siblings (conceived from the same sperm donor as my daughter), who had never met Mallory, but all of whom were deeply saddened over her death, and eager to learn about her life. It is as if, in the aftermath of my daughter's death, a village of love and support sprang up around Mallory and me. And from within that village, gratitude for my daughter's short but impactful life, as well as anguish over her death beg to be heard.

Contained within these pages are letters to my daughter who both in life and death, touched people all across the life span. Some whose lives she impacted understandably chose *not* to share their thoughts in this small book. But the contributors whose love and grief line these pages hope to shed some light on what it can feel like to lose a friend or loved one to suicide, and to address with honesty and respect the pain of those who, like my daughter once did, struggle to go on.

A self-inflicted death leaves a world of indescribable pain for friends and loved ones. Although statistics tell us that for every completed suicide, there are, on average, six to eight survivors who are deeply impacted by the loss, my own experience with my daughter's death tell me that those numbers don't even begin to tell the story. Throngs of people can be devastated by a single suicide, which in turn, can reawaken grief about earlier traumatic losses, as well as trigger thoughts or even acts of suicide in some of the more vulnerable survivors. The lives of suicide survivors are forever changed, and some will spend sleepless nights and restless days pummeling themselves with guilt and unanswerable questions.

Sometimes people suffering from severe depression think that no one would care if they were gone, or that the world would be better off without them. If that is how you or someone you know feels, the letters in this small book might help to keep me from answering, "If only you knew."

Mental illness is treatable. Depression is treatable. But the tunnel-vision thinking typical of severe depression often prevents people in its throes from even imagining a future more bright than their painful or unfulfilling past and present. Peggy Lee once crooned, "Is that all there is, my friends?" To the suicidally depressed, the future often tends to appear as a mere extension of past disappointments and traumas. Or perhaps they've run out of juice for living, or the thought of medication, therapy or life-saving hospitalization seems too stigmatizing. Because for all the people who work daily to help make this a more compassionate world for everyone, ignorance and fear about mental illness, plus the resulting shame and condemnation, still sadly exist. All across the globe.

Whatever the circumstances of your life, there are people who love and care for you, and who would do anything to help you live. *ANYTHING.* You may feel alone and insignificant, but you are neither. You are not your problems, your mistakes or your achievements. You most certainly are not your past. And, you are not others' opinions, mistakes or treatment of you.

As is the case with most suicides, the story of why my daughter took her life is complex and interwoven. That story is not contained within these pages. This book is about the unmistakable spirit contained within all life, and which is inextinguishable, even by suicide. It is about what we learn and how we go on in the face of deep pain, hoping ultimately, to shine a little light on the darkness.

It certainly was my intention with this small book, to honor the life and memory of my daughter. And if a single heartfelt sentence contained herein can help even one person to rethink their options and choose life, or to feel validated and understood in their efforts to come to terms with the suicide of a loved one, then I am doubly grateful.

~Lisa Richards

12

i carry your heart

i carry your heart with me (i carry it in
my heart) i am never without it (anywhere
i go you go, my dear; and whatever is done
by only me is your doing, my darling)
                    i fear
no fate (for you are my fate, my sweet) i want
no world (for beautiful you are my world, my true)
and it's you are whatever a moon has always meant
and whatever a sun will always sing is you

here is the deepest secret nobody knows
(here is the root of the root and the bud of the bud
and the sky of the sky of a tree called life; which grows
higher than the soul can hope or mind can hide)
and this is the wonder that's keeping the stars apart

i carry your heart (i carry it in my heart)

                    ~~e.e. cummings

14

Part I

Lisa's letters to her daughter

January 19, 2011

Dear Mallory;

Fifteen days have passed since I arrived home from work to find that you had taken your own life. And, fifteen days into my grief, I realize that I need to write to you. Unlike the months and years when we corresponded back and forth while you attended out-of-state treatment programs, or the twenty-one days you traveled up one side of Australia and back down, as a Student Ambassador, *this* time, you will not be writing me back.

I nonetheless have so much to say, so much to ask. And, when I found myself speaking to you in the shower today, I knew I simply wasn't ready to stop talking to you.

I talked to you for the better part of nine months, while you were in-utero.

I talked to you when you were a pre-verbal newborn, and I listened to your babbles and cries.

For eighteen years, we've conversed, occasionally argued, laughed and cried, you and I.

In our letters, cards and poems over the years, we've shared our deep love for each other, pieces of our personal journeys, chit-chat about friends, pets and family. Hopes and dreams.

Now, my only dream is to have you back. To wake up from the nightmare that has become my life. But you said your final Goodbye to me in a letter dated January 3, 2011. That Monday night sometime before or after we watched sit-coms on my bed with our rabbit Misty resting in her hay box, you popped your head out from behind your bedroom door and asked me, "Hey, Mom, how do you spell 'extraordinary'"?

You were writing your Goodbye letter to me, and I was naively helping you spell-check it. Had I asked you what you were writing, would you have told me the truth?

The tower of lies you built in the weeks and months before your death, and which can only become known to me in pieces now, as I weep and sleuth my way through the remnants of your destroyed life, suggests you were not willing to let me—or anybody—in, that the revelation of your secret, downward spiraling world would not avail itself in sufficient time for anyone to save you.

But *again*, a mother can dream.

The morning after you wrote your Goodbye letter to me, you said you had a sore throat, and therefore you weren't going to school. You turned down my offer of Throat Coat tea, but you asked me to warm some potatoes I had roasted the evening before, with garlic and olive oil. We sat together at the table, you eating your potatoes, and me drinking my decaf. I said, "Do you think this would taste good with yams instead of baking potatoes, Mal?" I knew you had most recently been open to the idea of yams, minus the marshmallows and cranberry sauce, and you answered,

"Umhmm."

"I'll try making it with yams, next time."

But you already knew there wasn't going to *be* a next time. *For anything in this world, for you.*

As I prepared for work, an hour or so later, you said, "Give me a hug." After we hugged in the short hallway in front of your room, I started for the front door, and you said, "Wait. Hug me again. "

It would be the last time that I would ever see or touch you alive.

At approximately 5:00 P.M. that evening, when I returned home from work with two small grocery bags, I knocked on your bedroom door, heard nothing, opened the door and turned on your light.

I found you dead.

I screamed, and a neighbor, the kind woman next door came running. "Call 911," I implored her. Frantically, I pulled your lifeless body down onto the bed from the crouched position in which I found you, and I tried in vain to resuscitate you. I breathed and breathed into your mouth. Your eyes, inches from my own, were opened and lifeless. Your blue mouth hung open.

And I—well, *I* was fired up on pure adrenaline and hysteria.

Within minutes, fifteen police officers and paramedics moved throughout our small home. I would later read in the police report that the paramedics pulled you onto the floor in your room, so that they could work on you. One police officer was ordered by another to open the clean white envelope addressed in black ink and perfect penmanship to "Mom" and with a pink heart sticker on the front. It lay visibly atop your desk. At some point later, as they wheeled your lifeless body on the gurney through our front door, a police officer told me that the letter would be given to me at the hospital after they entered it as evidence of your suicide.

As I wept in the living room, my hands shook . "Take *me*," I cried, looking upward at the ceiling. "Take *me*, and let my daughter live." But you had already made a bargain with God, and my vote was never even counted.

Not this time.

As we waited for Erika to arrive (a policeman asked me to call her, so that I wouldn't have to go alone to the hospital), I remembered that from behind the love seat in the living room, Misty was hearing the commotion of me weeping, policemen talking, and walkie talkies going off every few minutes. I asked the police officer who stood with me there, if I could please put the rabbit into her cage in my room while they worked on you, so that she wouldn't be so traumatized. But the answer came back *No*, (this could have been a crime scene for all they knew at this early stage). Hours later, after we left your remains (do you have any idea how difficult it is for me to write the word 'remains' next to 'your'?) at the hospital, and Uncle Ken and I returned in a stupor to our home, I cradled Misty for long stretches of time across my bare collarbone until her teeth chattered. But, little good it did: two days later, she would drop dead on her favorite patch of carpet between the living room window and the love seat. And what I would first notice on her small, gray, lifeless body in a nod to the last bit of you, would be her lips gone blue.

Erika arrived, just before the paramedics wheeled you out of the apartment, and she and her boyfriend drove me to the hospital. I leaped from his car the moment Kenny pulled into a space in the parking lot, and Erika had to yank me back. "Wrong entrance, Sweetie," she said. "Let's go this way."

Within minutes, the female doctor and nurse entered the small room where we waited. They didn't need to speak: I looked at their faces. You were gone.

When we went to you, you were covered up to your neck in a white sheet on a cold metal table. There was a tube in your mouth. The shock of this sight still coarses through me, fifteen days after your death, and it will become one of many flashbacks I will have for months and no doubt, years to come.

Me, Erika and her boyfriend stood there around you, and soon, two grief counselors arrived. They bore silent witness to our shock. Aunt Rita and Uncle Hal, Uncle Ken, Mali and Brian arrived. Mali kept approaching the metal table where you lay, looking at you, then shaking her head and backing away. She is a mother of two grown children, and she saw this from a mother's perspective.

I sat beside you, stroking your long soft hair, whispering occasionally to you, "*Oh, Sweetheart—.*" Your vacant eyes had frozen, half-opened. I kissed your eyelids.

Uncle Ken called Uncle Ron with the news. Disbelief was in the air, we were gagging on it. I would hear weeks later, in a conversation with someone from the hospital, that several emergency room workers wept about your death. The doctor who pronounced you dead has teenage children. Only the grief counselors were saying with their gentle faces, *Yes, this is death and she is gone. Accept the change.*

But I didn't *want* to leave you, or accept that you were gone. Can you understand that? We were there at the hospital for hours. *Open your eyes, Sweetheart*, I kept murmuring to myself, while looking at your lifeless body. *Please open them.*

In 2007, I feared we'd lose you—three serious suicide attempts is enough to push any parent over the edge. But then, we gave you treatment. And you gave yourself a chance to turn things around. You worked hard. In August, 2009, you graduated high school and came home. We moved to a two bedroom home in a complex dotted with red brick walkways and three story pine trees. Wildlife and waterfalls. I hoped that nature so close at hand would do both of us some good. I soon bought peanuts in bulk at Costco, and you and I laughed often, about the squirrels' daily feeding frenzies out on our patio.

You started school, moving your way through the theater arts department. It was hard trying to make friends at a commuter school after being out of state and in treatment for nearly three years, but you tried. God knows you tried.

Your heart ultimately broke in three places. And, more than that, you felt ostracized.

If only I had known how lonely you felt inside. But what you shared with your therapist, your two best friends and me over the past year and a half since you returned home, was an understatement—and a sanitized one at that—of the agonies you bore in silence.

And I had no idea that you were teetering on death's doorstep for five long weeks before it welcomed you.

I have puzzle pieces, now, but it's too late to fully complete the picture of your secret life that helped to bury you.

Did you leave me behind to tell the story?

At approximately 10:00 P.M., the night you died, my phone rang. It was OneLegacy, an organ donation center, reminding me that you had signed up at the DMV, back when you got your learner's permit, to donate pieces of yourself in case of death. Could they take your pericardium? The skin from your back and thighs? Your eyes? Bones from your arms and legs? Your heart valves?

I was still so deeply submerged in shock that you had killed yourself, but others' lives and health were at stake here. At some point in the man's extensive interview with me about your medical history, however, he determined that your risky behavior during your 2008 runaway to Venice Beach, eliminated you from the donation pool.

Is it selfish and shameful of me to admit that when I discovered we could keep your remains fairly intact, I was relieved? You don't need to answer that, Mal. I just did.

The day after you died, Uncle Ken and I started arranging for your burial. There would be a memorial service on Sunday at the cemetery, and we crossed our fingers that the coroner would release your remains in time. What a thing to hope for.

Danielle's family visited me late into the night on Friday, and Ashlie came too. The girls combed through boxes of photographs for a photo montage Danielle's brother Chris would lovingly put together in haste (well into the wee hours, I believe) and which his parents would deliver Saturday morning before Ken took me to the mortuary to bring your burial clothes. Your body went to its final resting place wearing grey pants, socks, your favorite black Vans, and your black knit sweater with rows of beige Irish lace around the collar. That last item made me think about a year ago when you selected it at a clothing store at the mall, that your fashion taste might be changing.

"We all couldn't believe how young she looked," said the mortician, who's a mother of three and whose eyes filled with tears as I told her about you.

I forgot to notify a lot of people about the memorial service; and still others, I would not know how to connect with for months. It wasn't for lack of desire to contact these people; pure and simple, I was, I believe, in those first days after your death, disassociated from myself as well as from the world around me. A dragging zombie, I did things by rote. Clean the litter box, feed the cats. Breathe. Sip water. Did I call your former voice teacher already, to tell her you were dead? Was it Wednesday?

Did I care?

On Sunday morning, nearly two hundred people sat in the large chapel. Photo montage images of you over your eighteen- year life span flashed across the screen to the sound of *Life is Beautiful*, by Vega4. And, if you are wondering why I did not linger at your casket after I placed the red rose on top of it while everyone watched: First, I was afraid that if I stayed there much longer, I might burst into tears, embarrassing myself, and further devastating the already shell-shocked crowd. And honestly, I also feared that I might try to climb inside the coffin with you. Grace, if I showed any microscopic measure of it that day, clung to me by a mere frayed thread.

You carefully planned your death around my work schedule. Your clothes hung neatly in your closet. You shut off your phone, discarded most of your schoolwork from your year and a half at Santa Monica College (except those few assignments that remained on your laptop). Thankfully, you left your journals, the cards, letters and poems we exchanged, poems and other writings you completed in high school and college, notes to and from the Tooth Fairy, some correspondence to and from friends, the photo albums I made you for your fifteenth birthday, dozens of loose photographs of you smiling and mugging for the camera in happier times, and the school projects you proudly brought home from elementary school. Jewelry, DVD's and CD's, including your favorites: Rent, Juno and Taylor Swift.

Three or four days after you died, I was sitting on the floor in your room, and I saw on the carpet about three feet from where you died on your bed, the flat gold charm with the pale pink flower and the words, "I Love You," that I had given you on a gold chain about a year and a half earlier. Were you wearing it when the paramedics pulled you onto the floor? Or?

Things. Momentos. Pieces of you.

Love,
Mom

January 21, 2011

Dear Mal;

I gave Ashlie and Danielle whatever they wanted from your jewelry armoire. I did keep the heart-shaped charm necklace I bought you at Sea World when you were three. The one with the blue dolphin painted on it, and your name. I wear it almost daily. I mailed or gave trinkets to Mary Simun, Mali, Erika, Aunt Rita, Ken and Alyson. The bulk of your snow globe collection went to your little cousin, although I brought your therapist the globe from Palm Springs, and your psychiatrist the one from Montana.

I kept your thermal tees, two flannel shirts and several other assorted pieces of clothing. But I also knew you would've wanted me to donate some of your clothing. Two trips I made to the Torrance Salvation Army, with your remaining clothing folded up in large plastic bags had me doubled over in physical agony for days. In fact, every time I have entered your room, for any reason whatsoever, I have felt something akin to Braxton Hicks contractions deep within me, just like the ones I felt over eighteen years ago before I went into actual labor with you.

Because—and call me unapologetically unenlightened, right now (that shoe fits just a little too well)-- I cannot release you with ease.

I love you,
Mom

January 23, 2011

Mallory;

You are everywhere. I cannot drive down a street, from Torrance to West Los Angeles, without remembering being there with you. I look at the passenger seat in my car—and picture you there, smiling at me, or saying, "Mom, can we stop at Subway?" Or both of us taking turns asking the other, "How was your day?"

You are walking with me through the supermarket, saying, "Mom, we need apples. And graham crackers." Now, as I enter Albertson's, I mutter under my breath to you. I say, "Mal, I cannot fathom being here without you." I see tortillas that you liked for your after school quesadillas. I see bananas, and those frozen Morningside vegetarian sausage patties that you loved. In the baking supplies section of the store, I find birthday candles for the nineteenth birthday you will never see.

On another day, I see you emerging from the top floor of the mall in your work uniform.

Everywhere, I hear you, I see you. But you are not here. And I don't really know how to be in the world right now without you somewhere on this earth, safe and alive. Because for eighteen years, you were my world.
You still are.

Love,
Mom

January 25, 2011

Dear Mallory;

No more college tours or family vacations.

No wedding to give you (that is, if you would want one).

No holiday ever again, for you.

No healthy love relationship that you spoke of, wished for.

No more Starbucks holiday pumpkin scones that you loved.

No college graduation, or graduate school that you said you were seriously thinking about.

No more road trips.

No more family, friends or animals who adored you.

No car (I was on the telephone the morning of your death, and told you so, about getting myself a used, certified Toyota, so that I could give you my car).

No more sleepovers at Danielle's, or Frozen Yogurt Thursdays with Ashlie, or hangouts with whomever at the clubhouse with the fireplace going.

No more letting me help you with your pain.

No more me rushing home to hug you, saying, "Hi, Beauty," then hearing you reply, "So glad you're home—give me a hug--I missed you!"

No more me looking forward to having a meal, a movie, anything with you.

No more Aunt Rita asking, "What does Mallory want for Hanukah?"

No more you feeding the homeless, which you consistently said you loved doing.

No more opportunities to get you the medication we now clearly know that you needed.

No more helping to save your life. *Certainly, no more of that.*

But then—

No more loneliness or broken heart or loss (except for us who now grieve losing you).

No more waiting for anything.

No more colossal depression or unbearable anxiety.

No more tears.

No more shame about your entirely human suffering.

No more lessons to learn or teach from deep within the School of Life. Yours are from another dimension altogether now.

I need to talk to you about Major Depression. It is treatable. In your non-depressed, or at least non-acutely suicidal state, you knew that. But once your feelings of anxiety and deep depression took you over, you had no interest whatsoever, it seems, in the possibility of light at the end of the tunnel.

You just wanted out from the intense pain. Death for you, in that dark desperate state of mind, seemed your only viable option, and you weren't going to give anybody a chance to talk you out of it. Suicide was your default button. And you pushed it.

I could not have known in my conscious mind what was happening here, in those final weeks with you. But it is largely the things which registered deep in my subconscious mind, about those last five weeks with you, and which I either overlooked or failed to see with clarity, that keep me up at night now, or drifting compulsively to thoughts of you slipping away. The snippets of conversations with you about various future plans—how your eyes would sometimes uncharacteristically dart away for the briefest second before returning to look at me; how your former resilience in the face of even big disappointments had started to wane; how I begged and begged you on that Sunday before you died, to please tell me what kind of outing you wanted to go on with me (in lieu of visiting Deerpark Monastery that day because I feared in the rain we'd be doing an outdoor meditation retreat covered in mud—how I wish we had gotten mud-caked now) but you kept saying, "No, you pick—"

Because the mind loves to Monday morning quarterback the past. I tell my clients about this often, when I catch them in the act of berating themselves for not living like they have a crystal ball at all times, with which to see the future.

But then again, there is mindfulness, and well, if I had been paying attention to you in those last five weeks with enough

of it, might you not still be here today? Or is this just me, bargaining again, and not "accepting the Now?"

Could a mother, so raw and unhinged in her grief over her only child's suicide think or feel differently?

Love,
Mom

January 30th, 2011

Dear Daughter;

I bring fresh flowers to your wall crypt each week. It was ivory roses one Friday; on another it was red and gold. Soon, I will put a crisp spray of deep blue silk irises and one pink gerbera daisy there as an occasional stand-in for fresh. But always, at least for now, I weep, sitting on one of the stone benches there. I weep for you, for all that you forfeited in exchange for freedom from your agonies. But yes, I also weep for me, and for the friends and family who ache for you, and who want to know, *Why?* This isn't a guilt-trip, Mal, just a friendly reminder of how connected we all are.

My tears at the cemetery generally form a quiet rivulet down my face (I know now to bring a handful of Kleenex with me from the car). But honestly, when no one is around, there are times when I sob out loud. So I am grateful that the Friday mornings when I pay most of my visits are a secluded time there. It is generally just me, and, somewhere far away on the grounds with shovels and equipment, or traveling the cemetery roads on electric vehicles, the burial guys. Most of them have heard your story by now, because as one of them explained to me the other day, "Your daughter was so young when she died, that well, we all just kind of heard about her." They are reverential, as well as helpful with ladders and flower placing as needed, being that "you" are four tiers up.

Last night, I fed the cats, ate a bowl of cereal and climbed into bed at 7 P.M. My mind feels simultaneously like a lump of Jello, and a battleground. Will I ever return from the battlefield, or simply grow more accustomed to living on it? And can I even fathom someday making a contribution to this earth? Wasn't your precious life my greatest contribution?

Have you found the peace which so evaded you at the end of your life? Erika keeps insisting that I helped you live longer, with all the treatment. Aunt Rita said that I left no stone unturned to help you. But did I? Was your loneliness abetted by growing up without a father, or was that a story planted in you by my own worries and fears? Throughout my days and nights now, pictures of multitudinous moments with you, from birth to the day you died, appear in my mind's eye, like a long, disjointed movie of our lives together, in which different motifs are emphasized at different times. Some scenes bring exquisite joy. Others evoke silent admonitions: *What the Hell was I thinking?*

And always, I remain haunted by my failure to know in the end that you were merely *acting* all right, even as you slid off the edges of the earth.

But I was also thrown off from your deadly plans by your socializing with friends as well as me over the Christmas Break— and by your dismissing of my few voiced concerns – looking back now, was all the visiting, and celebrating a kind of final hurrah because, well, deep inside of you, you knew, *This is it?*

Or, were you trying to tell me what was raging internally in the only ways that you *could* communicate, under the circumstances, and I didn't get it? You did indeed make two references to death, several weeks apart, but these references came to me as intellectual curiosities: one, you asked on your way to Danielle's house, another was you questioning the possibility of an afterlife one evening after dinner, as I stood in the doorway of your bedroom. Your therapist told me, in our first conversation after your death, that under the circumstances at the time, with the information that I knew about you then, I could not have known these were clues to your suicidality.

But, a mother should know. A mother *wants* to know.

It was as though you were speaking to me in Portuguese, with an occasional English phrase tossed in, but I was listening in Russian. And suicide has its own language, private and final.

I talked by telephone to your first therapist in Utah. Of all the kids she treated, she said (and this was echoed by the other therapists I contacted), you were not one she fathomed would ever kill herself. She cried with me. I thanked her for helping you to live.

Uncle Ken and Aly, Rita, Hal and I met at Juniors Deli today. Uncle Ken had a matzoh ball so legendary in size, that he photographed it with his phone and immediately loaded it onto his Facebook wall.

As I read the menu, I kept seeing things I knew that you'd like—a veggie sandwich on whole wheat toast, with fries or fresh fruit, perhaps? Some lemonade maybe?

At a nearby table, a cute young girl with braces and long, wavy brown hair sat with her parents and her grandparents. All I could think of, looking at her (but trying not to stare), was you. You missing lunch at Juniors, and us missing being here with you.

And then, of course, there's Valentine's Day around the corner·· and the red and pink aisles loaded with cards, candy and holiday trinkets at CVS or Rite Aid have me craving Pepto Bismol. I used to buy you a small stuffed animal or book each year, a bit of chocolate, and some admittedly mushy card from me to you.

I will need to train myself to be thankful instead, for all that we have been for, and given to each other, over eighteen years. You cannot find it at a store, because it isn't boxed or contained anywhere on this planet. Either are you.

Love,
Mom

February 4, 2011

Dear Mallory;

You and I had spoken recently of going to see *Hair* and *Spring Awakening* at the Pantages. You said, "Yes! Let's go!"

We talked of taking a family trip to Europe like the one the Lews did, within the next few years.

And, we were discussing plans to visit U.C.S.B. as a potential back-up to UC Santa Cruz, and because you said that you at least wanted to see the campus.

I am moving from the home you and I shared, into a smaller place. It's sensible, of course, but not having a room for you feels strange. The home we shared is filled with happy memories of you/us, such as the Sunday mornings when, awakening from sleep, you ribbed me for watching Joel Osteen on television in the living room, before we dressed and went out for Sunday brunch. Or, you sinking into your favorite living room chair and asking me, "Had any interesting patients lately?" Those were happier times before your depression and isolation took you over.

And this has now also become the home in which I found you dead.

Love,
Mom

February 8th, 2011

Mal;

I must have read several dozen articles and websites on suicide over the past few weeks. The internet, which can be a treasure trove of resources on Younameit, can also be used to discern the most lethal, least painful, and least likely to get you discovered before you're dead, ways to kill yourself.

At some point in my macabre reading fits, my stomach grinds and I must turn away from all this. Invariably, however, at this early stage in my grief, I also return to it. It is, in a perverse way right now, a connection to you. A way to try and make sense of how your broken mind might have fueled your final, irreversible act.

God knows how your therapist, with a new baby, deals with this. She said to me on our first telephone call after you died, "I know how Mallory felt about you, and I just keep asking myself how she could do this to you." If anything, from reading your post-Thanksgiving journal entry, I realize that what kept holding you back from your final exit, was the fear of hurting those you loved.

But we wanted to help with *your* hurts, Mallory. *You were not in the world to live for others*—except maybe for just a little while, until you could again find your own viable reasons for being here.
Your therapist tells me that you promised her countless times during therapy, that if you had suicidal thoughts, or found yourself to be struggling for any reason at all, you would tell or call someone--me, her, a friend, a hotline.

Yet days after you left us, I found a small, laminated white card with emergency telephone numbers including the Suicide Prevention Hotline at the bottom of your pink and lime green decorated Hope Box. Does it even need to be said at this point that you never called them?

Tears fall like rain as I come across your school yearbooks, and boxes of school projects you did over the years, minus the large painted insect you did I think, in preschool, and which had the bug's insides filled with different shapes of raw pasta you glued onto it. I kept that one in our back garage on Amethyst Street for over a decade, and when packing up to move us to the West side, I found a poor dead rat lying on the dusty garage floor, and half the pasta gone. *Time for this one to go*, I told myself. I had also tossed out the conical, three foot high green construction paper and glitter-glued Emerald City we made as a backdrop for your Wizard of Oz themed party—the one at which the Cowardly Lion looked so real that one little boy, upon arrival at our home, burst into tears and we quickly had to get the lion out of his costume, to calm the child down.

Because this is how it goes for me now: in and out of a dreamlike state in which I almost question whether the eighteen years we shared really happened—although the evidence of it (minus you) is everywhere. My love for you howls in every fiber of my being. You are, and always will be part of my every breath. Still, the part about you suddenly not being here in the physical world makes the present moment seem unreal to me right now, and strangely transitional. But, transitional to what?

I made a time line of your final five weeks of life on a giant slab of poster board, with everything relevant or possibly relevant that I could think of. It included every outing I
could recall you or you and I going on, over the holiday break; and I added to it the unfolding lies I started to discover after your death (like you no longer attending your math class from December forward; and your texted lie to me on December 14th, that your induction ceremony for

Phi Theta Kappa originally scheduled for December 17th, had been postponed until January); Your odd, uncharacteristic irritability, then leaving the house to meet friends for two straight nights at Hanukah's onset, and after which, with a coy smile, you made a sudden demand for latkes; the hurts by peers which you discussed with Ash, Danielle and me, but never hinted were hurting you as much as we now know they did; and your Christmas Day poem about being tempted to kill yourself—the poem you kept hidden in your journals and left for me to find only after you died.

Ashlie and I have talked for stretches of time about our disbelief that you are gone. Coping with your suicide factors prominently into Danielle's adjustment to her first year at UCSD— could it be otherwise? And Mary cries daily. But, I am guessing that as you slid away from us, so too did your ability to hold onto the love and devotion of all whose lives you impacted.

As I go through kitchen cabinets, to prepare for moving, I find: the madeleine cookie molds I once bought, knowing that they were your favorite cookies. I was going to veganize them. It never happened.

How could you not allow me to help you *this time?*

Are you in death a mirror to our failures?

Love,
Mom

February 12, 2011

Dear Mallory;

There are children everywhere. Teenagers, young adults, and little girls and boys talking and laughing with their parents. The sights and sounds of life and family.

The bittersweetness of both appreciating, and missing those joys, envelops me.

I have flashbacks. In one, I picture you making your final walk from the hallway into your bedroom, closing the door (did you say Goodbye to Misty and the cats?), then sealing your fate in your last moments alone. The other flashback that visits me often, is the memory of me arriving home, and finding you dead.

I cannot fight the flashbacks, so I just try to be still and let them come. It admittedly sometimes feels in this early stage of grief as though these haunting images could swallow me whole.

As for my own thoughts of dying, they are at this point daily and compelling. My Survivors After Suicide group leaders as well as my therapist tell me, *This is normal for what you're going through.*

These thoughts become a kind of comfort for me: I will not have to endlessly endure this mortal pain of missing you and aching for all you've given up. Of course, my more than scant recent readings on the afterlife (I'm a grieving mother—can you blame me?) suggest that if death isn't indeed the end, but rather a transition, then I will take every loose end with me. Homework for the road, so to speak.

Erika attended an event at a museum recently. While there, she saw paintings that depicted death frivolously. And it angered her.

From a list of intentions I wrote down on July 8, 2004:

1st line item: I will make certain that my daughter knows how loved and adored she is by me every day of her life.

By January 3rd, 2011 however, it seems pretty clear that that adoration had slipped from your radar.

On second thought, reflecting upon your Goodbye letter to me, you *did* know. It just wasn't enough.

Love,
Mom

February 13, 2011

Dear Mally;

In the flurry of paperwork that arrives from the Coroner's office, you are a "decedent." But you are *my daughter, my loved one.* A loved one who bought herself, incidentally, a navy blue vinyl lunchbox for school approximately six weeks before she died.
Forty days after your death, there is, even now, an almost constant feeling in my chest, akin to the sensation of a motor running.

The biggest, deadliest lie you told, was that you were okay.

She had so much potential, numerous people say about you. *She was one who was going to change the world.*

They are right, but in a way that none of us could have imagined: Only now does it become impeccably clear to me that in death, you have become a mighty teacher of suicide prevention.

Love,
Mom

February 17, 2011

Dear Mallory;

Days after you took your life, I noticed that the Pink Ladies, Honey Crisps and Fuji apples had been piling up in the refrigerator. That was a sign that something had been wrong. In earlier times, I couldn't buy them for you fast enough.

If grief can make a person crazy, then I have daily moments of feeling five point restraint certifiable. I walk around, at times, feeling as though half of me (or more) isn't even here. When I am not working, I talk to you, and think about you constantly. It is one reason, frankly, that I generally withdraw from the world these days. The other reason is that well, I just don't feel like being around other people right now during most of my free time.

In the past seventy-two hours, Ken, Rita, Ashlie and your psychiatrist have called me. Did someone voice concern?

I love you,
Mom

March 14, 2011

Mallory;

What else that could have impacted your safety and well-being did you lie to me about?

What was real?

Your love for me, and my love for you.

You are everywhere on the walls inside my new home: photographs, your tiny handprint at age six, pressed into ivory clay and tied up with a royal blue grosgrain ribbon at the top, for Mother's Day of 1998, your love poem to/about me, circa 2002, and my poem of encouragement to you that I wrote and sent you when you went to treatment in 2007.

Yesterday, you were memorialized at Hand to Hand where you fed the homeless, and they lovingly included me in that.

Aunt Rita is bouncing back from severe dehydration that put her in the hospital, and I am bringing her food, checking in on her and Uncle Hal. Erika has tendonitis. These things remind me that we all suffer.

Mally, at the end of your life, I sometimes thought that you were exasperated with me (and why wouldn't a teenage girl sometimes be exasperated with her mother anyway?)

But I had it all wrong. You had grown exasperated with life.

Love,
Mom

March 17, 2011

Dear dead daughter;

Where are you?

Are you?

Love,
Mom

March 21, 2011

Mallory;

A friend whose life you impacted more than you knew, visits you at the cemetery. Soon, they will put a marker on the wall of your crypt. It will read, in addition to your name, birth and death dates, "Adored daughter, Cherished gift to the world."

Will our spirits meet again?

You will forever be eighteen years and five months old.

Danielle passed her calculus final and reminded me it was International Pi Day last week, for which you ate pie with her last year.

I will never be a grandmother, but I will always be your mother.

As I re- read the letters you wrote to me over the past few years while you were in treatment, I come across one in which you wrote, "Thank you for giving me a second chance at life."

Love,
Mom

March 24, 2011

Dear Mallory;

I spoke by telephone with your kindergarten teacher. She'll be lighting a candle for you at her church next week.

I was grateful to connect with her. We reminisced about the jug of cooking oil, frying pan and twenty pound sack of potatoes I lugged to her class for Hanukah latkes when you were six. I thanked her for the love and enthusiasm she showed you from your first day of school.

I read the Facebook comments from friends of yours, flummoxed by your death. They hail you as *The One Everyone Else Always Came To With Their Problems*, and *The One Who Knew Life Gets Better*.

What happened?

I love you,
Mom

March 30th, 2011

Dear Mal;

In today's mail, I receive: An AAA card in your name. "Congratulations, Mallory Richards, on your free associate membership with AAA, for successfully completing our Licensed to Learn Teen Drivers Training Course." The card expires on January 15, 2012. One year and eleven days after the day you died.

Oreo has lost almost thirty percent of her body weight and Dr. Pott says she is in early kidney failure. We found a wet food that she likes, and I am feeding her on demand. She sleeps in the crook of my arm, her tiny head peering out from beneath the comforter. Cajun would make you laugh: He has taken over Midnight's old position as family protector, and howls (almost) like a dog in the middle of the night when a neighbor's cat dares to walk by our window. And, I have extremely happy memories of you buckling Misty into her rabbit harness and walking her along the path beside the narrow ponds where we live. *Thank You, Mallory, for showing so much love to the animals in your life. Thank You.*

As time marches on, I am able to bask more and more in extraordinary gratitude for you and your powerful presence on this earth.

Love,
Mom

44

April 1, 2011

Mallory;

I had dinner with Erika tonight. We were at BJ's, where we had your eighteenth birthday dinner just last August. Walking to our table, I remembered that night, when you saw through my surprise on the way to the restaurant. You looked beautiful to me, in your lavender pork pie hat and beige dress with the orange and white Indian bead belt. The photographs we took there that night would be some of the last pictures I would have of you alive.

Erika is going to Thailand. We talked about your upcoming Celebration of Life.

Each day, I reflect upon all that I wanted to give to, and do for you. And the ache in my heart remains deep and low.

Do you remember April Fool's Day, years ago-- you were about thirteen-- and I pulled into the Torrance McDonald' drive-thru, telling you with a straight face that I was going to order a hamburger? Vegetarians that we were?

You had a look of genuine concern upon your face, that said, *But Mom, you'd be eating an animal.* When the ruse was up, and I drove off without actually ordering anything, you howled with laughter.

Those are memories to cherish. That is the life in you that not even death can stop.

I love you,
Mom

April 5, 2011

Dear Mallory:

Ninety-one days you are gone now.

I need to bring the best of myself to others—my love, my peace and my compassion. All of which are merely an extension of my love for you. And some days I do this far better than others.

Did I let go of you, or did you let go of me? I realize now, that although so many saw you as wise beyond your years, there was also a frightened little girl inside you, aching for love and acceptance, hard-pressed to speak up on her own behalf (in spite of me teaching you as a pre-verbal infant, the language of feelings) and who somehow, could not see or touch in the end the love that wanted to enfold her.

You cut yourself off from inner and outer resources.

I know strong-willed, resilient people who still weep about your death.

Love,
Mom

April 8, 2011

Mallory;

I wanted to buy you galoshes for the rain one day, remember?

You said, "Yeah, they're okay, but they're not for me."

That is apparently how you came to look upon your life in the end.

Love,
Mom

April 12, 2011

Sweetheart,

I pretty well know your taste in guys by now—sensitive, with or without big glasses, offbeat handsome. And the other day, a colleague's client was sitting in the waiting room of our shared offices. He smiled at me, and I thought to myself that had you seen him, you would've said to me privately, "Hey Mom, he's soooo cute!"

Mary told one of her classes yesterday, "You guys have to be nice to each other." She was thinking of you,spoke anonymously of someone she knew who's no longer here, and who had felt deeply hurt by people she loved. Mary broke down.

The class was stunned silent.

And I won't lie: It's difficult, planning a celebration of your life that ended in suicide, instead of planning with your input, your nineteenth birthday party or getaway. But, your illness chose death, for you. So, at this point, what else can I do? To *not* celebrate your precious life isn't an option.

The food will be cruelty-free in your honor, the paper goods will be turquoise and purple (the colors for suicide prevention), and the goodie bags will include enough suicide awareness paraphernalia to keep us all on alert. For the next time somebody's suicidal loved one tries to fake us out.

And, I am hearing from several donor siblings of yours. They mourn your death as well as never having met you. They e-mail me pictures of themselves. They have your eyebrows. Your eyes. Your gorgeous hair. Might knowing them have helped to tame your loneliness, and to give you a firmer sense of yourself? Or is that just me, bargaining again? My grief about the donor siblings you never met before you died has had me racked with subhuman wails for days.

Yet, this: A team in your honor is shaping up, for the September walk/run for the L.A. Suicide Prevention Center. *You are everywhere, still.* And, in my better moments, I begin to truly understand that that's how it is, with Spirit.

I love you,
Mom

April 20, 2011

Dear Mal;

We've had some warm weather days. The kind of day which, in earlier, happier times, might've had you by the pool with your books and cell phone.

The cats make concentric circles around me in sleep.
Danielle wrote me a letter, and it reminded me of you and I writing to one another across the miles.

I am learning to function in spite of and through my grief. Slowing down when I can, helps. Hot baths, most definitely. And lots and lots of herbal tea.

Yesterday, Aunt Rita's dog Rinni ran out her front door, left open by a worker, and he dashed down the street where poor Aunt Rita saw him hit and killed by a car. Our need to let go is everywhere, it would seem.

Yet, returning home at night from work, knowing you are not there for me to hug, or say, *I missed you* to—well, let's just say it's an adjustment.

And sometimes, spasms of maternal guilt and pain bear down on me like sharp knives falling from the sky.

Mother's Day is around the bend, and Danielle has invited me to a Long Beach tea house.

Today, the news featured a story of a man whose mother's ashes were lost at a post office, preventing him from scattering them at sea. There are rituals and actions which become meaningful and necessary in the wake of grief.

Aunt Rita will eventually get a new dog, she says, from a rescue group.

It is loving myself at this difficult time that comes the hardest.

Love,
Mom

April 22, 2011

Dear Mallory,

I finally started back to exercising this week. It's strange—there are select songs on my iPod that are neither too cheery or chipper—which I can still listen to as I run.

I know that your perfectionism entered hugely into your suicide.

You keep receiving invitations to take another Student Ambassador trip.

And P.S. Do you even *know* how many bags of cat poop I need to carry out each week, without you?

Love,
Mom

April 24, 2011

Dear Mallory;

Today I took Aunt Rita and Uncle Hal to Marmalade Café at the Grove to celebrate Aunt Rita's 81st birthday.
You might have eyeballed strangely my dry grilled artichoke with lemon wedges minus the aioli, but I did enjoy it.

Last night might well be the first night since your death that I remember you coming to me in a dream. I heard in my sleep the theme song to The Sound of Music, the one musical which propelled you early on, into a love of theater.

I worked for over twenty years as a grief counselor, and then you killed yourself. Kind of takes things to a whole new level, doesn't it? And, there are clients who have told me throughout the years that I helped to save their lives.

But in the end, I didn't save *yours*.

Did you research how to die on the internet?

Love,
Mom

May 2, 2011

Mallory;

There's an online rant site where depressed people post about their struggles, and some post their Goodbye letters before killing themselves. I looked back into their archives; you did not post on the site even incognito before you killed yourself. I respond from my heart, to two or three posts daily, trying to instill a tiny ounce of hope. Trying to do for them what I can no longer do for you. Mary goes on the site, responding to posts also.

I still sleep some days more than I ever have before. But I figure that there are far worse things I could be doing with my grief.

I love you,
Mom

May 4, 2011

Dear Mal,

Can I tell you how much I miss just picking you up from school?

If this world were a more compassionate place, or if I had built you stronger, I keep thinking that you might still be here.

And, if you could see the outpouring of love for you here in the world, I know it would move you.

I love you, Sweetheart. You were on the cusp of adulthood, and didn't think that you could make it.

Now, in my darker moments, I wonder if *I* am going to make it. Without you alive in the world, sometimes, quite frankly, I'm not so sure that I *want* to make it.

For such is the pain body of grief.

Love,
Mom

Mother's Day

Dear Mallory;

So Danielle took me to this amazing little tea house that I know you would have loved. Against the far wall of their tiny gift shop, are rows of cups and saucers, in beautiful designs. You pick out the cup and saucer you want to drink your tea from. Then(and this part is optional), you enter a hat room. I passed on the hats but Danielle picked out a cute, wide-brimmed straw hat for herself to wear.

The server brought steaming hot pots of tea, kept perfectly warm in tea cozies. There were scones with clotted cream, trimmed bread sandwiches, a soup and dessert even. It went on and on. We talked about your celebration of life, Danielle's experiences at UCSD, her trip to Belize, her family, and you. *Of course you, and always you.* A sweet young family sat near us, all dressed in their Sunday best, a dad, a mom, and a son and daughter. That made me miss you with a vengeance. So my cloth napkin came in handy as a tear soaker.

With gratitude, I receive telephone calls from Aunt Rita, Erika and Uncle Ken, as well as a call from one of my clients with several grown children. And with gratitude, I reminisce about eighteen glorious Mother's Days that you gave to me.

I love you so,
Mom

May 21, 2011

Dear Mallory;

I am re- reading Tolle's *A New Earth.* It helps to keep me rooted in the present moment, but in all honesty, continued longing for you to still be here in the flesh, yanks me back away. *At frequent intervals, still.* This is the roller coaster of grief I've so often spoken of to my clients, only now it's *me*, gripping the sides of the car, hanging on in any way that I can.

I uploaded *No More No Less* by Mercy Me and Brandon Heath's *Your Love* onto your Facebook page, because I think of you when I hear these songs, and hope that some of your friends will like them.

I find myself wondering: How much longer on this side of eternity will I be? The answer comes in a soft whisper: *As long as I need to, to learn and teach the lessons of my daughter's life and death.* For this has now become my destiny.

A toe I broke several weeks ago is healing nicely, in large part because of the less than stylish brown flats and gray ballerina shoes I have been wearing to work instead of heels. And, I think to myself: Broken bones are so much easier to recover from, than this godforsaken grief.

I miss: Getting a $1 nondairy soft serve ice cream cone with you at the mall, every few weeks or so. *And so much more.*

Love,
Mom

May 22, 2011

Mal;

After talking to your spirit for over twenty minutes today while sitting on my bed, an epiphany comes, and it defies all manner of doubt:

You were holding the *I Love You* charm from the necklace I bought you in your hand when you died.

And, my shameless sobbing in the cocoon of my small new home now becomes relentless.

Love,
Mom

May 29, 2011

Mallory;

I took Aunt Rita, Uncle Hal, Alyson and Uncle Ken to Vintage Tea Leaf today, for a belated celebration of Alyson's twelfth birthday. I wondered briefly if a Victorian tea house would be just a bit too prissy for your uncles.

They loved it. Aunt Rita and Alyson loved it.

Uncle Ken donned a wide-brimmed pink velvet hat.
We drank Scottish Breakfast tea, English Breakfast tea, Lemon tea and Decaf Marsala Chai tea. I drank me a river. And, there was something very cute about seeing Uncle Hal eating a dainty trimmed bread sandwich.

I love you "to the moon and back" (as we often used to say to each other when you were small). My precious daughter, you have given so much to me. And you now give me a red carpet of sorts, to eternity.

I vacillate between patience and baited breath to make the trip.

Love,
Mom

June 10, 2011

So, girl.

I've been instinctively drawn towards flocks of birds, and trees with lavender flowers since your death.
And I am starting to think that maybe I can be okay.

Remember me stocking up on a ridiculous amount of Von's vitamin waters about five years ago when they went on sale, our inside garage on Amethyst Street taking on the appearance of a bunker storing supplies for the next great natural disaster? You laughed heartily at me. A mother planning for the future—and God forbid we should be without our $. 99 mineral waters.

Today, down the corridor from where your remains lie buried at the cemetery, I saw a single water bagel inside a sandwich-sized baggie hanging from someone's wall crypt. A loved one was honoring a dead person, with an actual bagel dangling on a mausoleum wall. And, on another wall, bottom row center, a beige *"I Love You Darling Husband"* card taped atop someone's marker.

What we do and don't do to honor and remember the dead.

Love,
Mom

June 12, 2011

Dear Mal;

I'm exercising more regularly, to prepare for the Suicide Prevention walk/run in a few months.

Danielle texted me—we'll work on plans for your Celebration of Life over dinner on the 26th, and, earlier that day, I'll take Uncle Ken and Alyson out for brunch and to a movie.

Life's inanities, such as incorrect cable bills, or the rare late-night, fired-up ghetto blasters of youthful neighbors slip past me like grains of sand through my fingers: Losing a child to suicide, well, you've pretty much hit a mother lode of loss and change. And there's just no small stuff to sweat anymore.

Whisper, like Oreo, is in kidney failure now, in addition to the IBS he has battled for years, so I am basically feeding him on demand also. Not to mention putting chopped up pills at the back of his throat: one for appetite, another to prevent vomiting. And, a gooey gel onto his tongue, to up his potassium count. It's a veritable pet hospital I've got going here.

The other day, I saw a strawberry plant growing outside the Santa Monica office building where I work. And it jogged a memory of being with you at Wilderness park one afternoon, years ago when you were about nine. We were hiking around the park and saw a rabbit there. A plant ripe with berries grew nearby, and you asked my permission to offer one of the berries to the rabbit. I helped you pick the berry, and as you held your hand perfectly still with my coaching, and gently offered the treat to the rabbit, he/she cautiously leaned over, then bit you, nervously mistaking the tip of your finger for part of the berry, before hopping away with your juicy gift. You burst into tears. You were trying to make a kind offering, and then felt punished for doing so. I understood as your mother at that moment, that *that* hurt you more than the actual chomp of the rabbit's teeth on your finger.

Looking back now, it seems that this had become a theme in your life in too many situations, in the years before you died: You, holding out offerings of loving-kindness to others, only to be disappointed or hurt.

But what haunts me now, is this: Was it also a theme that I failed to protect you from harm? Or that my own distorted view of myself before I saw myself through the ample, forgiving lens of spirit and soul, spilled onto you? Or that my needs and limitations as a single working parent too often left you, as an only child, lonely and invalidated?

See how far-reaching grief-guilt goes?

Yet, in brighter moments, I have admittedly felt your loving presence more often lately, and it helps, if even for a brief moment, to calm me.

I love you,
Mom

July 4, 2011

Dear Mallory;

So it turns out—and I only realized this recently-- that Independence Day is the six month anniversary of your suicide.
Is there darkly humorous comedic irony in this?

I have fond memories of taking the shuttle bus on the afternoon of July 4th with you, year after year, from the Del Amo Mall in Torrance to Wilson Park, where, among the throngs of frolicking kids and families, we'd carve our territory with a giant blanket, set down our picnic basket and petite thermoses of decaf (for me) and soymilk hot cocoa (for you); you'd dance or sway to the music, and we'd rove among the craft booths for trinkets (early on, you gravitated toward fairy crowns and wands; later you graduated to mood rings and glow-in-the-dark necklaces); we rode the train through the park when you were a toddler, and always, you'd debate pretzel versus American flag- colored popsicle or such; in more recent years, you'd howl as I'd cautiously shuffle toward the next available Port-A-Potty as if I might not emerge from its smelly recesses alive. But darkness always came, a hush would fall over the massive crowds, and we'd huddle close to each other on our blanket, hearts and bellies satisfied, as we watched the awesome beauty of the fireworks exploding above.

You *loved* our Wilson Park Fourth of Julys. And now, as I try to marry my steady ache for you with a bit of mercy, I receive this memory, and all others that have become my bounty, with humble thanks that I ever had you in my life to adore at all, and to celebrate life with.

Love,
Mom

The deeper that sorrow carves into your being, the more joy you can contain. Is not the cup that holds your wine the very cup that burned in the potter's oven?

~Kahlil Gibran

July 30th, 2011

Dear Mal;

Today, at a Santa Monica cemetery, I attend a balloon launch sponsored by Compassionate Friends, for parents who have lost a child. It does not matter how they died: accident, illness, murder or suicide. Some died in utero before they even had a chance.

We are members of a club we've been inducted into, kicking and screaming. Some of us also comprise a Venn diagram of sorts with the Survivors of Suicide parents whose children killed themselves. And with both groups, there is a certain freedom that I feel, to be myself. With both groups, there are tacit things that I share. So there is a bit of comfort here today, for me, for a while.

Potluck refreshments are served on a long table against a wall of the mausoleum. We are eating among the dead.

Pastel-colored ribbons attached to a cluster of helium-filled balloons dangle at eye level in the mausoleum vestibule. We each take a balloon, and write a message to our loved ones on its rubbery surface. I write: *Mallory Erin Richards. You are here. I am here. I love you.*

There is a brief program of music and poetry readings. We sing Amazing Grace.

We are then invited to stand on the grass nearby, and release our balloons into the open sky.

I've read that they can travel as much as five miles upward.

For some reason that I do not understand at the time, I wait just a moment, until after the other parents have released their balloons, which cluster together and move gently in an angular pattern farther and farther into the sky. It is a warm day, and there are no real winds blowing.

I release my balloon. And, swear to God, it soars at a breakneck clip. It moves in its own direction, past the other balloons. I watch it shimmy into the sky, then disappear on its own.

It's the first time in my life that I ask myself whether a balloon might possibly be imbued with your personality.

Love,
Mom

64

August 8, 2011

Dear Mallory;

Today would have been your nineteenth birthday.

In the clubhouse yesterday, we celebrated your life. Twenty-four people arrived for a brunch in your honor. They viewed a suicide quilt hanging in the north east corner of the room. It had memorial squares dedicated to twenty people who took their lives before you.

Who left loved ones decimated with sorrow, like you did.

I put up photo displays of you looking happy and very much alive, from infancy, until just weeks before you died.

The guests received goodie bags containing:

An individually wrapped Lenny and Larry's lemon poppy seed cookie

A suicide prevention pin

A purple and teal silicone Suicide Prevention wristband

Information about the L.A. Suicide Prevention Center and their upcoming fundraiser

An inspirational stone with words like *Love*, or *Trust*, or *Faith* or *Family* carved into it

A photograph of you smiling, at age seventeen

A tiny teal tube of bubbles and a bubble wand.

Christine Hernandez and her mom Laura surprised us all with large suicide prevention pins they made by hand with satin ribbons and small satin yellow flowers glue-gunned in the middle. Uncle Hal even wore his pin on his lapel to a doctor's appointment today, where the receptionist commented on its beauty, inquired about its significance.

The guests at the celebration of your life were humble and respectful, because it was *that* kind of event, and you were *that* kind of person. We played music both from your ipod and from me having combed the air waves for months, in search of songs that spoke to my love for you, and to the occasion. And *of course*, three Taylor Swift songs. Shortly after you took your life, I remember thinking to myself with stunned disbelief that I could not fathom you'd ever do *anything* to prevent yourself from rushing out to buy every album Taylor Swift will ever make, into her eighties, even.

As usual, I provided enough food for an army at this event, however I am not entirely to blame for this. You see, I was not familiar with Facebook, before you died. So, when over thirty people from your Facebook page RSVP'd that they were coming to this event, I didn't understand that not all of them would actually attend the event. If I had known, I only would have prepared enough food for *half* an army, and still would have had plenty of food to send home with people, a habit which as you know—or at least knew-- gives me great joy.

Before we served dessert, the highlight of which was vegan cupcakes from a downtown Santa Monica bakery, I invited guests to join me in a gratitude circle. One by one, we deposited stones (symbolizing the heaviness of grief) into a basket, in exchange for a small painted ceramic heart, as we said aloud what we were grateful for, about your life.

Tears poured down Alyson's face, and she clutched at her father while he spoke softly for the two of them. Erika, always the epitome of strength and rationality, couldn't get a word out, and quickly handed me the microphone. Your nanny Aura said you were like a daughter to her, and the raw grief on her face as her voice quivered extracted tears from almost everyone in the room.

Because your suicide is a real sucker punch to us all.

Today, for your nineteenth birthday, I will bring breadcrumbs to Polliwog Park in Manhattan Beach where you and I used to feed the ducks and birds when you were small.

I and several of your friends and loved ones committed to spend nineteen minutes in lovingkindness toward ourselves and/or others.

And, I will place a dozen red roses into the flower cup where your remains lie buried.

I love you, Sweetheart.

Love,
Mom

August 17, 2011

Dear Mal;

Tonight at my monthly drop-in Survivors After Suicide group, I tell my fellow group members that I feel as though I only have one less face than the three faces of Eve.

There's an adaptable side of me that works efficiently with my clients, and who can finally tolerate meeting friends for an occasional cup of coffee or meal in a restaurant.

The other side of me goes to a dark place from which the living may be hard pressed to return. This is the part of me that isolates, and thinks I am starting to know a little too well what you must have been feeling before you died.

And the two parts of me feel utterly disconnected, I tell the group. *Am I crazy?*

The group says, *Oh, no, you're not crazy. That's how it was for us. The first year after we lost our loved ones. Eventually, you will find that the two parts come together.*

Mally, do you remember when you were small, and we used to say to each other before we'd part for almost any reason at all, *Miss you need you love you want you?*

I miss you need you love you want you.

Love,
Mom

September 25, 2011

Mallory;

This morning was the L.A. Suicide Prevention Center run/walk. Fourteen people honored you with their presence here today, for "Team Mallory." Your picture was up there on the memorial banner with countless others, and seeing your smiling face with other suicides was deeply emotional for us.

At the event, Active Minds, a Washington-based nonprofit raising awareness about mental health issues for college students had their display of 1100 backpacks spread across a lawn, representing the roughly 1100 college students in the United States who kill themselves each year. And, so, after the walk/run, we roamed among the backpacks until we found yours. It has your laminated picture, as well as a brief narrative I wrote about what a wonderful human being you were. The last sentence I wrote was *What does my daughter's suicide invite you to think about?*

It is unthinkable to imagine 1100 dead bodies of college students who killed themselves in a single year, strewn across these lawns, like so many backpacks.

Love,
Mom

September 30, 2011

Dear Mal;

In the last two weeks, the U.S. Postal Service has delivered the following in your name:

~A mailing from ITT Technical Institute, offering to send you a complimentary copy of *Ten Things Every High School Graduate Should Know About The Job Market* and asking, of course, if you might like to attend their school

~A postcard from the Los Angeles Times, extending a time-limited offer to you, for 4 day a week newspaper delivery, for only $.75 a week

~A glossy brochure and personalized letter from the Assistant Dean of Admissions at Gonzaga University in Spokane, Washington, inviting you to consider transferring there to finish your Bachelors degree

~And, an Early Bird Discount from motivational speaker Anthony Robbins, for you to attend his *Date with Destiny* event in Palm Springs, California, from December 9th through 14th, 2011

Meanwhile, in an online survey I am asked to complete for a local business, I read this question: *How many children do you have?*

Love,
Mom

October 15, 2011

Dear Mallory;

Here come the holidays.

And, I am thinking about how to spend them in the spirit of your love. Giving back, helping someone in need, (and aren't *all* the living in need, *somehow?*) is what I keep returning to.

After the holidays, I will face the one-year anniversary of your death. And I have chosen to spend it in solitude. Some have said, *life gets easier*, and coping with daily living since your suicide has indeed become a bit easier over the months (at least in between the downward spirals). Yet in some ways, the longer you are gone, the more it hurts me. As time goes on, the less capable I am, of playing little head games with myself, like, *She's on a trip, and any day now, I'll get that call or text to pick her up at the airport.*

The longer you are gone, the more I worry that someone might forget you.

I won't let them.

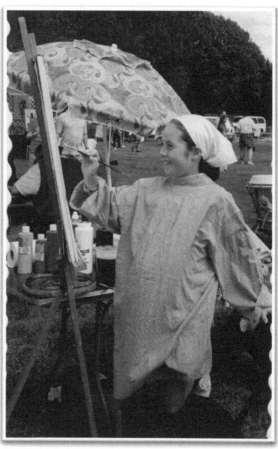

People come to my office, some of whom have suffered their own catastrophic losses, and my compassion for them is profound. Their brave attempts to cope and grow through their suffering inspire me.

You inspire me.

But Mom, I can here you saying from wherever you are, *I killed myself. How can you be inspired by someone who killed herself?*

Because neither your suffering nor your suicide will ever, at least for me, define you, daughter.

How you lived, defines you.

How you loved, defines you.

And before you lost your footing on this earth, you did both, admirably, generously. At the end, it was only *yourself* you deprived of your love. All of us who knew and loved you, are blessed. And you are the magnificent daughter I chose to love and adore.

Love,
Mom

November 23, 2011

Dear Mallory;

In the spirit of your compassionate nature, I loaded up my car last week with supplies for a family of five children whose parents were murdered in Mexico several years ago. When I read their story in the Los Angeles Times, I knew that I had to do something. I delivered my car load of supplies to the oldest boy at his place of work. I told him about you. I also brought coffee cakes for the staff and other teens who work there, wanting no one to feel left out. And, in a few weeks, I will bring this family another load of supplies in time for the Christmas holiday.

Last Saturday, I attended my first International Survivors of Suicide Day conference at Cedars Sinai Hospital in Los Angeles. I felt nurtured and understood. And, as I listened to other survivors whose hearts have also been broken open by love and pain, I thought to myself,

How can there be room or reason, or time for war? For the battle strategies of ego, which can only maim and destroy, when it is our love and compassion for ourselves and one another that finds answers, that unites and ultimately saves us?

At this, the beginning of my first holiday season without you, Mallory, I commit to honoring and commemorating your precious life in any way that I can.

I give thanks for eighteen years and five months of laughter, love and lessons. Of indestructible memories. I give thanks for your exquisite spirit that has touched lives and changed us for the better (starting with me), in good times and in sorrow. I give thanks that you were here. That we were here. You are the heart and soul of me, and whenever I despair, if I become very still, I can feel you whispering in my ear.

I'll never stop listening.

Love,
Mom

Part II

Letters to Mallory from Friends and Family

Uncle Hal, Mallory, and Aunt Rita

Mallory with her Uncle Ken at *Charlie and the Chocolate Factory*

*If we lift our eyes, to the moon, the stars, and sun; then might we hear
the ancient truth ~ in spirit, we are one.*

*~Frances Key, in the song,
"The Flag of Living Stars"*

Dear Darling Mally;

You and I met the day you were born. You were an exquisite, beautiful baby. You had rosy, perfect skin, and your hair seemed to be tinged with sunlight. You shone like a bright penny and seemed content. You were such a bundle of joy. I fell in love with you that day and forever more.

It was pure delight sharing your birthday celebrations throughout the years. Mother planned such wonderful birthday surprises for you--clowns, musicians or storytellers, plus games and treats. How happy you seemed, playing and giggling with all your friends.

Mallory and her Aunt Rita

Uncle Hal and I were mesmerized years later, watching you sing and act in plays. You were amazing in Charlie and the Chocolate Factory.

Mally, you were such a happy person as a child. It always seemed as though there was a ray of sunshine in and around you. You had many friends, and your life seemed to be filled with so many happy activities.

But in your teens, you withdrew. So many changes. I knew you had alot of painful, unhappy experiences. Mom and your doctors hoped to help you cross the bridge to better times, and you went away to school.

When you returned home in 2009, your past seemed too painful for you to talk about with me. But you and I had fun times together. Sometimes, mom would bring you over to my home on her way to work. You were a sleepy head. After you'd rest for a bit, we'd plan our day. We visited museums, and also Ocean Park Amusement Park, where we went on wild rides, held hands and screamed our heads off. You loved going to movies with me, shopping at the malls, and I'd let you pick the restaurants where we ate our lunches. I so enjoyed being with you, and I always looked forward to our days together. I have many wonderful memories of being with you, Mallory.

Now, when I shop in the stores that you loved, I turn around and I look for you. Mallory, you are not there. I want you back.

My darling Mallory, you left the world too soon. I often feel your spirit is with me, and perhaps you are with us, in a different way. Maybe you are an angel looking down.
I love and miss you, my beautiful Mally.

Love,
Aunt Rita

76

Dear Mallory,

I first met your mom almost sixteen years ago, when she had come into my store in Redondo Beach, to order cookies for your third birthday party. Your mom impressed me with her kindness, intelligence and compassion. I told her I wanted to meet you sometime.

The first time your mom brought you to my store, you appeared with painted fingernails, and wearing your mom's high-heeled shoes. You made us laugh with your sense of humor. You were so cute and sweet that my employees couldn't get enough of you. We asked your mom to bring you back to visit us.

Once in a while, when your mom was shopping nearby, she came into my store with you. One day, you asked me if you could decorate a cookie. I put an apron on you, and asked you which cookie you wanted to decorate. You usually chose cookies in animal shapes. After several visits, you approached Penni, the store manager one day, and asked her to retire so that you could take her place! That's the kind of little girl you were--funny and sweet.

Over the years, as your mom and I became friends, she visited me sometimes at work or at home while you were at school. She would tell me how happy you seemed, and that you were doing well in school. She was very proud of you. And, sometimes, you and mom would come over to our home to visit or have dinner with me and Brian.

Later on, your mom invited Brian and me to several plays in which you performed. We marveled at your talent. Your mom supported you 100% in everything you wanted to do. After you went to Australia as a Student Ambassador one year, you brought Brian and me pictures of your adventures, as well as a small gift.

We kept in touch with your mom over the years. One night, she called us and said that you had been hospitalized after trying to kill yourself. We were devastated. Your mom researched how best to help you, and she finally chose a treatment center in Utah, to try and save your life. It was very hard for me and Brian to see you and your mom going through this. I am a mother of two grown children, and I couldn't have done what your mother did for you. She spent hours, days, weeks and months researching, conferring, planning and worrying about how to help you. She devoted almost every waking hour when she wasn't working, to helping you.

When you returned from out-of-state treatment, your mom again worried about your safety. Her strength throughout all of this was amazing to us.

Mallory, you were a loving, talented, caring girl who always saw the best in people. But, you were also naive. You sometimes believed in others' goodness and honesty to a fault.

For your eighteenth birthday, your mom invited us to a surprise party for you at a restaurant near your home. In hindsight, you seemed distracted, and as though you were acting a part in a play. The part of a young girl who's happy and at peace--but who in reality, was struggling.

In spite of your hard work, and others' efforts to help you, it seems that your suffering got the best of you at the end of your life.

Mallory, you will stay in our hearts and minds forever. We will remember you as we once knew you--the sweet loving girl you really were.

With Love,
Mali and Brian Erb

Brian and Mali Erb at *Alice in Concert*

Dear Mallory,

You cannot imagine how many times I have thought of you and your Mom over the years.

From the first time the two of you walked through the gate at Manhattan Beach Nursery School, I knew you were a tight team. Your mom embraced the early childhood philosophy that encouraged you to explore the environment, friendships, imagination, and even conflict. And you did it all. In many ways you seemed older (or maybe it was wiser) than your very few years.

At some point, you told your mom that you were afraid of "The Man" at school. Concerned, your mom asked you to point this man out. Well, it wasn't one of the dads as I at first assumed. It was barely 5 year-old Lucas (who, in all fairness, was large for his age). I made a commitment to observe the interactions between the two of you. "The Man" did tear through the yards with a merry band of followers, and beware those who crossed the bike path at the wrong time! What I noticed was that you were not singled out in any way, but would occasionally get too close to the action. You were attracted to the excitement, and seemed to want to figure it out, yet you were intimidated by his size, age, and energy. I think you wanted to observe but were trying to calculate a safe distance.

Mallory at Manhattan Beach Nursery School

Your mom and I even made a plan to talk to him and his mom one morning. When he arrived at school, his mom said he had had a rough morning, and it wouldn't be a good time. I wonder if you remember that you and I talked a long time about your feelings that day. You said that "The Man" was scary, and I told you a surprising thing about him. Even though he seemed so big, he still slept with his mom, and got very scared and cried in the night. I can still see your face with your big eyes and bouncy hair. You looked so surprised. The whole rest of the day you followed him around and even talked to him on the climbing structure.

The reason I remember this story so vividly, Mallory, is because it was such an example of bravery and compassion coming from the most adorable child. You were open to life, and to facing challenges. But more, you saw through a 5-year-old boy's bravado and met it with a 3½-year-old girl's heart. Now that was powerful. And I'll never forget you.

Karen Patterson
Former Director of Manhattan Beach Nursery School

Dear Mallory,

Remember me, your second grade Sunday school teacher? I am sad to communicate with you in this fashion, as I'd much rather look into those sparkling eyes of yours, see that vibrant smile and give you a big hug.

We met when you were about seven years old; you and your mom had joined our congregation as new members. Your Mom wanted only the best for you and she was the most involved and genuinely interested parent we worked with in our class. You soaked up the learning materials, wanting to understand the holidays and rituals, and, with that sweet voice of yours, you sang along with all the hymns. You partnered with classmates in our group discussions and competitions, and were equally at ease with the boys and the girls – rare qualities for someone that age.

We invited you and your mom for dinner when our daughter was an infant. You took note that our pond turtle was eating live mealworms. This disturbed you. You felt that the worm was of equal value in the world, and did not deserve to be raised as "food." When we explained that this turtle breed was a carnivore, you understood, but were simply not satisfied with this answer. It wasn't fair to the mealworm! To us, it was clear that you had a level of compassion and an analytical mind far beyond your years.

We were honored to see you perform in several plays in Redondo Beach. You seemed so at ease on stage, and getting into character seemed to come naturally to you. After one play, Marci and I took a photo of you in your Geisha girl costume, in the backstage area of the theater. Your smile was from ear to ear, your eyes beamed. You loved the stage and it loved you right back.

In later years, at your mother's 50th birthday celebration, you explained in detail all the vegan Chinese dishes to Marci and me. During the dinner, I filmed you on camera reading aloud a special message to your mother. It was heartfelt and emotional. You displayed what a wonderful young woman you were becoming--mature, confident, poised, well-adjusted, and capable of achieving so much. Before the party, I had scanned in many photos of your family for a slideshow, so I was able to see the love that you had for your mother, and for the many pets you lived with over the years.

I know that you accomplished much in school, and traveled internationally at a young age. You represented the best the U.S. had to offer. Marci and I knew you were on the road to happiness and success.

A number of years passed... We knew that a rough patch in your life sent you on another, darker path. My wife Marci and I were concerned, but we knew that your Mom would see to it that you did not face these challenges alone. We were hopeful that the news would be positive down the road.

Sadly, when I received the next call from your mother this past February, I knew in my heart that you had made an irreversible decision about your life. I know that you would want your time with us to be of value to others, and I'm sure that it will be. If anything, your suicide shows me that even someone with a solid network of family, friends, teachers, peers, and a religious education can fall victim to helplessness and despair. When my daughter is old enough to fully grasp the scope of this situation, we will sit down and share your life with her. We'll make sure she knows that she is of more value on this earth than floating above it. As much as I want to be angry and sad about your suicide, I look to my own little girl. I see a similar set of sparkling eyes, and a vibrant smile like yours. I know that the future of this planet lies with her. My hope is to use The Story of Mallory Richards to inspire, challenge, guide and nurture my daughter on her own successful path.

As our liturgy says in the Blessing of a Child: "May God make His face to shine upon you...may the Lord grant you His Peace."

With Love,

Gary Eizenwasser
Sunday School teacher

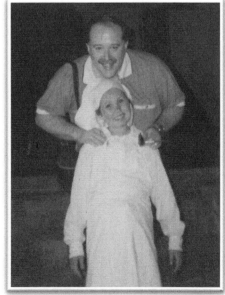

Gary and Mallory at one of her plays

Mallory and Erika

Mallory,

It's hard to know where to start, in writing a letter to you. I've missed the deadline by over a month, trying to avoid the feelings this brings up in me. At times, I am mad at you for what this has done to your mom. There's a part of me that believes no matter how hopeless it seemed, no matter how much you hurt, you shouldn't have done this to her. You took the way out that seemed right to you, but you devastated someone else in the process and that's not fair. I know in my heart that you were trying to spare her. The "I love you" charm, the suicide note were all designed to send a message of "I love you" and "this isn't your fault". I guess at 18 you think you can make it easier with those little gestures...but you didn't.

I am 100% positive that your energy lives on, just as mine will and your mom's. I also know that you are present with us; that you are experiencing our grief; that you are comforting your mom but not in a way she can feel. You have a bigger picture now; a "universal view" so to speak. I don't believe that emotions such as regret or grief are part of our energy after we pass, however, I believe you are part of a greater consciousness and awareness that influences the human spirit, and you profoundly understand the pain a suicide brings. I challenge you, Mallory to make a difference in the world by influencing the living human soul. Show us how we can make a difference on an individual and personal level. Be with me to remind me to be kind and understanding when I may be rushed or insensitive.

Remind me that when I think I'm mad, I'm actually just hurt.

I love you Mallory. I always think of you with your shy, engaging smile, with your absolutely gorgeous hair and your beautiful face. You were an angel then, and you are an angel now. I think of you often with my sweet girl Rainbow. I know that death is not the true end of anything and I know I will see you again; until then I will miss you. Comfort your mom. Help her feel your spirit. Give her the knowledge that she will share her spirit with you again someday. You owe her that much at least ☺.

So no goodbyes...just until we meet again. I know that time will be sooner than we think.

Love,

Erika

Mallory and Tsedale

Hi, Mallory;

It is sad and difficult for me to know I am writing you a letter that you will never get a chance to read. But I am writing you this letter so that your legacy of being so kind and helpful to others, goes on.

Do you remember the time you and your mom rescued a small bunny rabbit? I still hear your voice—you were so excited. And then months later, you kept telling your mom, "Our bunny needs a friend." You had all these reasons that your rabbit Winter shouldn't be alone... so you and your mom adopted another rabbit, Misty.

Mallory, you were the sweetest, kindest person I have ever known. When I first met you, you were about seven years old. I was renting a room in your home. You said, "Welcome to our house, and this is for you." You handed me a toy panda bear. Then you introduced me to your many pets. You said, "We have six cats. This is Cinnamon. She is kinda shy but she is so sweet. This is Oreo..." You went on to describe for me the unique personalities of all your pets.

It was pleasant for me to live at your home, and I was happy and grateful to have you be in that part of my life's journey.

Mallory, your manner, kindness, politeness and sweetness show how well you were raised. I always believed that you would grow up to be a fine woman and a good citizen. Recently, you had been in my thoughts. I said to myself, Mallory was so smart, honest, outgoing, and assertive when she was young. Knowing her, I said to myself, she might be in one of the finest universities in the country. But all that changed in a single telephone call, when your mother told me that you had killed yourself. I was shattered. I asked, HOW? WHY? Mallory, you were smart enough to differentiate between safety and danger. How unfortunate that you became trapped in the darkness, with peer pressures. And you became part of all the craziness.

Mallory, why didn't you go to your mom for help in that crucial second before you took your life? I know that Lisa would have done anything to ease your pain and save you from the tragic path you chose. Your suicide is a powerful lesson about how dangerous choices, peer pressures, and depression can help to destroy a beautiful soul. Mallory, you have taught me that our fates are decided by the choices we make. I am so sorry for all the pain you had to go through. I wish that I had had a chance to tell you how lucky I was, to know you as a person. You were a beautiful, bright star who became broken by extreme pain and dangerous choices.

With Tons of Love,

Tsedale Abebe, August 7, 2011

Each friend represents a world in us, a world possibly not born until they arrive, and it is only by this meeting that a new world is born.

~Anais Nin

Dear Mallory,

You were one of my best friends growing up. I remember you always having a smile every day at school. You were a happy girl, nothing would ever bother you; you didn't keep grudges and you were friendly to everyone. I have vivid memories of spending time at your house, playing with your cats. "Midnight" was the name of one of them, and he was clearly my favorite. In addition to having many cats, you also had a couple of rabbits. Since I didn't have any pets, it was nice to

Aleena and Mallory

spend time at your house and play with yours. For the day, I could play with Midnight as if he were mine, as if he were part of my family. I was able to feel this way because you let me. You understood that I lacked the relationship that you had with your pets, because that's the person you were. That's the person you are. You were so generous, and you sympathized with others. Even more, you cared for others. Not only did you care for people, but you also cared for animals. I was so amazed at how one girl can have so much passion in her.

Unfortunately, in the fourth grade, my family and I moved to a different city. It was difficult, as I was very attached to my friends. After the move, our communication slowly lessened. The distance was hard; I was at a new school and had to acclimate to new people. Although, now that I reflect on it, that isn't an excuse. I greatly regret not keeping in touch with you, I greatly regret not being there for you. You were a great person and friend, and had an even greater heart.

Mallory, I know you are looking out for all of us, just like you always have. You will always be in my thoughts. Just know that even though we lost touch, I haven't forgotten you, and I never will. When I think back to my childhood, you were a huge part of it. I will never forget those memories or the great moments we spent together. Thank you for giving me the best childhood. I love you and miss you.

Aleena Virani

Dear Mallory,

When I think of you, I remember a sweet, innocent girl who was free-spirited, kind, and one of the most genuine girls I have ever met. You were a normal kid, and fun-loving. I remember going over to your house in the summer, playing with your cats, and watching Disney movies together. Sometimes, you would come to my house before or after drama camp, and we would hang out and make charm bracelets together. You were a typical little girl, wanting to run outside, play with animals, and simply enjoy life. You were talented and so much fun to be around. You were words that I can't even describe. You were one-of-a-kind.

I remember a shirt you used to wear. It had a picture of four animals, and it said, "These are my friends, Don't eat them." It was the cutest shirt I ever saw, and you wore it when we were young. Your loving spirit spread to every being on this earth, including animals. You were the only vegan girl I knew, and you did it because you truly cared about the animals. Some people thought your shirt was silly and teased you about it, but you never said a word back. You just smiled and walked away. Once, you wanted to change what you were wearing, because of the teasing, but me and another friend told you to ignore the people teasing you. You felt better after we talked to you.

Mallory, you never seemed to have enemies. You never gossiped about others, and only spoke kind words. What hurts me the most is that you didn't seem to know how amazing you were. You always doubted your singing talent at drama camp, but we all thought that you sang beautifully. You doubted your appearance, but we all thought that you were the cutest thing we had ever seen! Everyone can agree with me about what a great person you were, Mallory. And it didn't take your death for us to figure that out. Although towards the end of your life, you seemed unaware of how much you have impacted the lives of those who knew you, I hope you see now how special you have always been to us. I wish that I could have told you more every day how talented and spirited you were, because of the pain you must have felt toward the end of your life. It hurts me to know that if someone--anyone--had just let you know how much you meant to us, you might be alive today.

Mallory, my mom and your mom always got along. You and I thought it was awesome that our moms had the same first name, and I think we also each had a cat with the same name. I remember your mom making us sandwiches, or something else yummy! Your mom was always around, and was super sweet like you, Mallory. My heart goes out to your mom. I cannot imagine what she goes through every day, since you died. I hope your mom knows that so many people care about her and pray for her all the time--even people she may not even know. My whole family is here for your mom. She was so sweet, and such a giving mother, as well as a loving person. Although I was not around your family for the last few years, I hope your mom knows what a great mother she was to you, and that your death is not her fault. I cannot think of another mother who was as sweet and genuine as your mom, Mallory. We all love you so much, and we love your mom too, very much. What I loved about you and your mom was your kindness--it almost made me feel like a part of your family.

When I found out that you died, Mallory, it hurt me more than I ever thought it could. I don't know why you took your life, but sometimes I wish that I could go back in time and let you know how special you were. I wish that I could have made a difference in your life, and helped you to reconsider your actions. I wish I could've told you what our friendship meant to me. I would have done anything for you, even though we hadn't talked in years. You deserved everything in this world--a great life, friends and happy memories.

I cannot even describe what a great friend you were to me. You always listened, and wanted to help others. I really miss you, Mallory, and your presence will be with me forever.

Your death has taught me how precious life is, and that we must treat everyone as if they might not be here tomorrow. You have taught me to be a more loving person, like you. I hope that one day, I can be as genuine as you were. I hope that in heaven you are looking down on us, and that you can feel our love, because we all do love you very much. You were a one-of-a-kind, special little girl and your presence will be with me forever.

Love,

Alyssa

Alyssa and Mallory

Dear Mallory,

Do you remember that time in Drama Camp when Pam was teaching all of us how to be lady-like? You were the only one in the group on stage to be wearing a skirt, and you were the only one to actually sit down and stand up in a modest, lady-like fashion. You are one classy gal, Mallory. I loved spending time with you. You always had an interesting story to tell, a fun joke to spin, and you were just all-around lovely to adventure with. I am really sorry that as we got older, we would plan to hang out, and were always "just about to" hang out, instead of actually getting together. That makes it especially hard for me to believe that you are gone; we still are "just about to" hang out. Next time you are free, next time I'm home, next time we're in the same place.

I miss you darling girl,
Arielle Schwitkis

P.S. We should hang out soon.

Dear Mallory,

I first want to start by saying that I miss the hell out of you. Since the day I found out about your suicide, I have been so confused about why you chose to do this. I remember how we met in Girl Scouts and became great friends. You were such a happy, bubbly person; I loved to be around you because it was always a great time. We have had some good memories. I remember that we would have these Girl Scout Tasting Bees, where we dressed up and made food from the countries we represented. That was so much fun. I even remember the three countries we represented--England, China, Spain. I miss those days. I also miss going to each other's houses and spending the night at one another's homes. Sometimes, when I spent the night at your home, your mom would make the best potato patty things. I don't know what they were called, and even if I did, I wouldn't know how to spell it. But anyway, it was always a great time at your house with all your cats and oh I can't forget your bunny. You liked arts and crafts, so we would always make so many things. Another memory I have is of water balloon fights in your front yard in the summers. Oh, so many great memories with you. I can't believe that I have known you for ten years. Time goes by way too fast. It seems like just yesterday, we were these two little girls, who would play and have fun like we didn't have a care in the world. Once we got to middle school we were friends, but I wish we would have hung out more. Then we got to high school, and it all changed. I saw you in high school but it wasn't the same because the school was bigger, and we were in cliques. Then, I remember not seeing you in 10th grade. I really didn't know why you left, but then you came back, and I saw you every once in a while. That was great, even if it was just five minutes in passing. It was nice seeing your smile and just saying hi. When I heard that you graduated early, I was shocked, and I was even more shocked when I found you on Facebook. This is how we kept in touch. I found out

Christine and Mallory at one of her plays

that you and your mom had moved, and was so happy for you both. I thought this would be a great change for you. It was great hearing from you, and we connected through Facebook from the eleventh grade, up to December 2010. Then one time, I was at the Westfield mall, and I saw you there, working. That was an awesome day for me; because it was the first time I had seen you since the 10th grade. Seeing you there made my day. It was a few days before Christmas. You seemed so happy. It was like I was looking at a happier Mallory. We talked about meeting up sometime after the first of the new year. But on January 9th, I found out that you had killed yourself. I was shocked and confused. I will never forget that day. I was walking by the beach at about 4 P.M., and I got many phone messages from different people. When I finally called one of them back, I learned that you had killed yourself. I was speechless. I really didn't know what to say or do. I cried. I stopped in my tracks. I went down to the ocean, and I just sat there and cried until the sun set. Finally, I walked home. I cried the whole way there, wondering why you would have killed yourself. To show my love to you, one or two days later, I walked to the beach with two friends. I had bought a candle and put your name, and birth and death dates on it. We watched the sun set and lit the candle. I had to do this for you.

I only have good things to say about you. Like, when you walked into a room, you lit it up with your smile and your bubbly personality. You have touched so many hearts. And so many love you and will miss you so much. I hope that you are in a better place and at peace. I will watch over your mom for you and will keep in touch with her. We are friends on Facebook, and we have made a page for you. She has posted information about events that celebrate your life and honor your memory. I will go to every single one of them. For your birthday, we will be celebrating your life, with your mom and some close friends. You will be missed and loved so much! Xoxoxo

With much love,
Christine Eustolia Hernandez

Dear Mallory,

Goodness. That is all I can say, *goodness*. I had no idea! I mean for godsakes, you were the last person who I expected would kill herself. Why? There was no reason. You were so amazing. Probably one of the most amazing people I knew. You were so beautiful, cute, adorable, talented, kind, caring and genuine. I loved being your friend so much. When you disappeared we all talked about possibilities, not because we wanted to gossip about you or stab you in the back, but we were genuinely worried. We wanted to know what had happened to our fun-loving Mallory.

When I saw you the November before you died, volunteering at the homeless shelter, I was soooooo excited. I don't think you understood how much it meant to me, to have us share that experience together. I was really, really planning on coming back to visit you because I really wanted to get back into your life again. I planned to go one weekend, and I was even going to message you on Facebook to tell you that I was coming. But then I got someone's text message that you had killed yourself. Shit, I was so confused. I literally could not believe that you had taken your own life. I mean, Mallory Richards, so sweet, innocent, happy, exuberant, not a sad thought in your mind. But I obviously did not really pay attention to who you were. I am truly sorry for that. I wish I could have been there to show you how much you were loved and appreciated.

I remember how often we brought up the time years ago, when we played hide and go seek, and you were the seeker. We let you look for us for so long that you gave up and thought we hated you. Mallory, whether you can hear me now or not, I could never have hated you. You made me feel so good about myself, and that is a special gift. People who can do that have an indisputably large, bright and beautiful heart. During one of the plays we did, I think it was A Mid-Summer Nights Dream, I had my birthday sleepover. We didn't really know each other that well until about a week before, so I invited you last minute. I remember you were so self-conscious about whether I really wanted you there. But seriously girl, I wanted you there more than anything. As a kid I did not hang out with people I didn't like, so inviting you was genuine. I really wanted to be your friend and I was so excited that we had grown close enough so quickly that I could invite you. And we ended up having soo much fun!

Sarah and Mallory at cotillion

I also loved how much we could bond over our vegetarianism. As a kid, I never found other kids like me, but it was so awesome to find you! And plus it was so cool to go to the same middle school. I remember that sometimes, I would stay behind, after 7th grade lunch to talk with you during 8th grade lunch ☺.

Every time I think of your name, I smile. I still find myself saying, "oh my friend Mallory did that with me, she was so good at it!" or "This one time, my friend Mallory and I....." I always loved spending time with you. Especially when you were Alice and I was Tweedle Dee, a match meant to be made. Thank you for always being the wonderful you that you are. I will forever miss you and your bubbly, contagious personality. Love you girl, and don't you ever forget that people always did and will always continue to do so.

Love,
Sarah

Mallory and her rabbit Winter

Dear Mallory,

I remember the first time I met you and your mother. You were so eager to help and we were so happy to have your help. As a youth volunteer, your sweet smile and demeanor while helping to run our charity gift shop was a pleasure.

I remember the day you showed up wearing flannel pajama bottoms, a t-shirt and Ugg boots. While this was not the usually gift shop attire, I took it to mean that you had become comfortable with us and that we had made a friend in you.

It is not possible for me to think of your passing without thinking of what it would be like to be in Lisa's shoes at this difficult time. I just cannot imagine losing my child. I too have only one child, and a daughter. She is older than you, and is struggling with severe alcoholism and depression. What I am learning in Al-Anon is that we cannot control the actions of others. We can only guide, then "detach with love". That is difficult to for me to understand how to do.

I know that you are so loved, Mallory. By friends, family, and most of all, by Lisa. I know your mother did every single thing she could possibly do to make you know that, and to help you want to stay in this life with us. It is difficult to accept that just because we are mothers, just because we love our children from the core of our beings and to the depth of our souls and then some, it does not mean we can save you from the emotional dings that the rest of the world may choose to deliver to you. We cannot save you from your own thoughts and actions that can take you from us. It is still up to each person to choose their own path.

I really wish you had chosen to stay here with us. But you didn't. So I will have to remember you as a rosy-cheeked angel in flannel p.j.'s and Ugg boots, with a bunny under each arm. Say hello to Winter and Misty for me. I will never forget you.

With much love,

Bona Tucker
President, PetSave Foundation

If the only prayer you said in your whole life was 'thank you,' that would suffice.

~Meister Eckhart

Dear Mallory,

I met you during my second year at drama camp. I attached to you immediately. There was just something about your radiating personality and smile that could make any situation better. I knew we were going to be friends. Throughout the summer we always had talks during camp and after, as well as creating subtle signals during the play to remind each other to smile and have fun. We were performing in Alice in Concert. You were Alice, and I was in the company, so we were almost always on stage together. It is a time I will always remember. There were times after camp when we would call each other from home, and talk for hours about almost anything in the world. I will always remember going to your birthday party at Seaside Lagoon. I only knew a few camp kids who were there, because I didn't grow up in Redondo Beach. But you made it a point, Mallory, to hang out with everyone equally, and to bring us all together. I met some amazing people there, who I wouldn't have met if you hadn't had us all mingle together.

Mallory, you impacted my life in a way that not many people really could. There was always something about you that would bring the biggest smile to my face. You had a positive attitude that made me want to be that way too. You did so many things that made me want to be a better person, strive to do my best, and love everyone and everything that ever came into my life. Today I feel the same way. I strive to do my best every day, even though there are struggles. I do what I can to help those in need and whenever I see a "Lost Pet" sign on the street, I keep my eyes open, so I can find the animal and bring it back to that family. I have to think that that is from your influence on me.

The one thing I regret the most is that more recently, you and I hadn't talked in the longest time. When you went away for treatment, it had already been awhile since I had seen or even spoken with you. When I heard that you were away, it made me really realize that I missed one of my good friends, and I wished I could have stayed in more regular contact with you. I remember one day, I was playing around on the computer when I came across a friend request on Facebook. It was from you. I was so happy that we were finally going to be in contact again. We chatted a few times, and talked about getting together, but there was never really a convenient time. When I found out about your suicide, I have been so confused about why you chose to do this. I was speechless. I can remember exactly what I was doing, who I was with, and what I was wearing when I got the call. I was shocked. I thought we had just chatted on Facebook not too long before. Your death turned on a light for me, that no matter how someone looks or seems, there could always be something down deeper. I have even thought about that with myself, because I can be a nervous wreck or worried about something, but people think I am completely fine. Your death made me realize how important it is to be honest about your feelings with yourself, and with those around you, because no matter what, the people in your life love you. Your death has made me believe that I need to let those in my life know that I will always be there to talk with them.

Mallory, I will never forget you. Your smile and your laughter brightened my life every single day. You were a true friend and I think about you often. The other day, I came across a tape from Alice in Concert and it brought back so many memories. Please know that you are always loved and will be missed. I love you.

- Alex Gryder

Mallory and Danielle

Dear Mallory,

Hey. That's how I always started a letter to you. No matter how long it had been since we last talked or saw each other, it was always "hey" because we could pick up and write for pages like no time had passed. We only met in high school (isn't that crazy)? We were in the same drama class freshman year. You were passionate about acting, and I was taking the class to get rid of my fear of public speaking. We got to talking, and pretty soon it seemed like I had known you all of my life. We could do anything together and have fun. Remember when the chocolate factory was closed so instead we went to the park, had a junk food picnic, and cheered for the family playing baseball all the while pretending that we were at a professional ball game? It wasn't even a nice day; it was cloudy and freezing, but that didn't seem to matter. Remember how, during the winter break before you died, we had a sleepover, and stayed up all night talking about our hopes, fears, dreams, struggles, random things, everything? I was sure then, that you would be the one friend I would have forever--"until we're 143 and have no teeth," we used to say. What did I miss? What was I not listening to? How could you call me your best friend and not feel like you could lean on me? Would it have changed things if you knew that every day, I cry (and so does everyone else) because you're gone? The songs from Rent (the last movie we saw together) haunt me. Didn't you know: "Without you, the ground thaws, the rain falls, the grass grows. Without you, the seeds root, the flowers bloom, the children play. The stars gleam, the poets dream, the eagles fly, without you. The earth turns, the sun burns, but I die, without you"? I'm trying to go on, because I know you wouldn't want me to be like this. I'm trying to be strong, but I'm just learning how deceptive strength can be. How couldn't I see that before? You fake it until you make it, knowing that strength is a sick illusion; the more people you fool, the more you start to fool yourself. But it's time to stop pretending that I'm ok, or that I even understand why you did it. Did you give me all of those calendars because you knew I would have to handle 2011 on my own? In your goodbye letter to me, you said that you didn't want to be so stuck in your head anymore, that it was internal, and that it wasn't my fault. But I can't help blaming myself. In that beautiful mind of yours, how could you not see how loved you were? Why did you let a few people make you believe that you weren't good enough, when there were so many more people who would do anything for you? What if I had called just before you were about to do it? What if I had attended SMC, and I wasn't so far away? What if I never missed a day of texting/calling you, to tell you how amazing you were? You knew that I would do anything for you. What if I didn't wait for you to ask? But my questions are useless. You aren't here to answer them.

Danielle

Dear Mallory,

I have spent weeks composing this letter to you, in my head and in my heart. It is nearly impossible to put into words on paper how I feel about you, and how much impact you have had on my life. I choke on these words even as I write them; they are woefully inadequate.

I remember the day we first met as if it were yesterday. You came bouncing into my room like a little ray of sunshine, bubbly and smiling all over. You were a petite little freshman just entering high school. It was before school started! You came in, introduced yourself and asked me if I would sponsor your club. I was surprised--I did not know who you were, and you wanted me to work with you. I asked you why you had come to me; you replied that you had asked around, and that I was the one you wanted. Wow. Ok. Unusual. You were not shy or discouraged. You plowed ahead and asked me to sponsor your vegetarian club. I gently pointed out to you that I was not a strict vegetarian, and you were not swayed. I told you that I was really busy (I mean, after all, you did not know me, and I was sure you could find someone better). You did not budge. I finally suggested, that since you were new here, you talk to a few other teachers first before making a decision; that perhaps you could find a better sponsor. If you still wanted me, you could come back again. You agreed, and after we chatted a bit, you left. I was sure I had not seen the last of your charming spirit; I was right.

You returned. You said you had made other inquiries and were certain that I was the one. How could I refuse? Obviously, I did not. I am so glad that I made the choice that I did (and that you did as well!). Had you not returned to me, had I not accepted your offer, I might never have known your shining little light. It was always a pleasure to see you, to work with you, to speak with you. I can't believe how much you have touched my heart. Again, I am crying as I type this. You had so much love, so much empathy for the little animals who could not speak for themselves. You did not care what other people thought; you were on a mission. I understand that mission. Mine was the whales when I was your age.

Mary and Mallory

I miss your laugh. I miss your smile. I miss you bouncing into my classroom all excited and passionate and full of energy and life. This is so hard to write. I can't believe how easily such a bright light can be snuffed out. It is simply not comprehensible to me. I wanted to see you grow up, go to college, and change the world. I remember the Animal Acres fundraiser like it was yesterday. We ran into so many obstacles, yet you refused to get discouraged. It was going to happen, and it was going to be a success, regardless of what road blocks got in the way. You were so driven and determined. Unstoppable. How could that lovely, sweet, darling light be gone? I miss you every day. I remember the conversations we had, many of which involved speaking about your extremely high level of empathy, and how I warned you to protect yourself from letting those intense feelings hurt you. I hoped to help you prevent some pain. I feel as though I failed in the worst way. I would have done anything to protect you, and you deserved it. If I had been fortunate enough to have a daughter, I would have wanted her to be just like you. I loved you then, I love you now, and I will always love you, dear, sweet, charming, lovely, bright, talented, giving, sharing, caring, precious, one-of-a-kind Mallory.

Mary Simun
Biology Teacher
Redondo Union High School

Dear Mallory,

This makes no sense whatsoever. Is this life? Am I dreaming? Why are you not here, breathing the same air as the rest of us? Instead, you're in a place where you go away and don't ever come back. You become nothing but bones. Your body goes away. That sweet smile I loved seeing every day in school—it's nothing but a distant memory now. I love you so much, girl. I miss you with all my heart as well. Mallory, there is not a single day that goes by that I do not think of you. Gosh, it's like someone wake me up from this nightmare I'm in. I mean if you, of all people could not make it in this crazy world, why should anyone else be able to? I mean *you, Mallory*, the one who was so brave, sweet and kind. The one who knew right from wrong. You were the one who knew that things do change and never stay the same. It was not suppose to end up like this. You should still be on this earth with the rest of us. I can't even begin to comprehend how I'm here and you are not. You were so full of life and passion for everything. Every person you ever came in contact with remembers you. You were just that extraordinary of a person. Sure I don't know the whole story about why you took your own life. I at least thought I somewhat knew you. Mallory, I considered you my sister, and I still do. For the rest of my life, I'm going to keep asking myself why you killed yourself. I wish you were here with me so we could share the memories that were yet to come. Since I have been in therapy, I have

Shelby and Mallory

learned that when people die, they most likely die with their problems. There is no escaping them, even in death. Mallory, you mean alot to me and I guess all I wish is for you to be happy. Please be happy in whatever way that may be. I know where ever you may be that you are making others happy, just as you did on earth. I wish you could have seen how loved you were and forever will be. You will NEVER be forgotten. Mallory you will forever remain in my heart. Thank you for entering my life......

Love Always,

Shelby B. (Eeyore)

Dear Mallory;

Your eighteen years of life have changed this sixty year-old woman forever. When I first saw you at Hand to Hand, I wondered, why is this young girl here in Santa Monica, assisting the homeless by serving hot meals to them? I *had* to be there, per a court order of fifty-five hours of community service, because I had turned right without stopping first, in my car one day. But you, Mallory, were there for the heart of it.

You were a ray of sunshine with your glowing red-blonde hair and mischievous smile. I liked the way you wore your hair relaxed in a side ponytail that swooped down the front of your shoulder. I used to think that this hairstyle was provocative, but on you, it looked so natural and innocent. So I have begun to wear my hair to one side on a regular basis. Before seeing you, I would only wear it that way on a special occasion. This is one of the ways you have changed my exterior life.

As you know, Mallory, we never spoke. In fact, I never opened up to anyone at Hand to Hand. I observed everyone chatting, but I stayed aloof and did not get to know anyone. I already knew a few of the people there from the Agape Spiritual Center where I am a Spiritual Counselor.

Mallory, your death has motivated me to come out of myself and to get to know those around me. Just yesterday there was a teenage boy at Hand to Hand, and we had a delightful conversation about food. Because of you, I am more open to conversation with people who I may never see again in my life.

I regret not having opened up to you to chitchat while you were alive. Might we have spoken about your depression? Your treatment for it? Would you have told me about how you attempted suicide three times? Would we have spoken about your love of theater arts, and the Redondo Beach Drama program that was cut, due to funds? Or, might I have told you how much I appreciated your presence, and how important your life is on this earth? None of us at Hand to Hand knew of your dark agony.

Mallory, it's a sad state of affairs that thirty percent of all teenage deaths in this country are caused by suicide. This breaks my heart. I was bullied for years, throughout grammar school. I was too tall, too plump, and unable to speak English. I was a poor immigrant from Buenos Aires who landed in Los Angeles when I was seven.

Mallory, because of you, I am now motivated to make it my life's mission to help reduce teenage suicide. In your short but powerful eighteen years of life, you gave me important values that have transformed my life. Thank you, Mallory, for your inspiration. Your essence lives in my essence forever.

Love,

Feliza

Dear Mallory

We were never good friends; in fact I can't really say that we were ever much more than friendly acquaintances. We shared one class over a year and a half ago, and we only spoke a few times. Yet, every time I ran into you after that class, be it in the bathroom, or outside the theatre building, across the way – I could always count on you for a smile and friendly greeting. Always.

When I think back to that class in the Fall of 2009, like many other classes I have taken, I can't remember the names of over a quarter of the students in that class. I'd probably only recognize about half. *But I remember you.* I remember your smile, exercises we practiced together, conversations we had, that beautiful poem you wrote and read to the class.

When I read over the messages that have been posted on your Facebook memorial page, I see hundreds of messages from people who loved you. I see messages from people who wish they could have had the opportunity to know you, and I see messages from people like me, who knew you very little, but who had obviously been touched by your presence in a very big way.

It makes me very sad to think that someone who has meant so much to so many people, could have felt so alone. My heart goes out to you for the pain you must have felt, and wherever you are, I hope that you have found the peace and happiness that you so deserve.
I will never forget you.

Suzanne Wood

Dear Mallory,

It's hard for me to know what to say, but I want to let you know that I really wish that I could have met you. Your mom only has the nicest things to say about you, and I feel like maybe if I had been able to talk to you that things might have been a little bit better, to know there are others kind of in the same place. Now, I can only imagine what it would have been like to meet you, but I look forward to seeing you one day, probably a long time from now. Your mother has been so nice to talk to, and you both seem wonderful. Even though I don't know you, I love you and miss you too.

Love,

Kate (your long lost big sis)

Dear Mallory,

The first time I had contact with your Mom was on February 15, 2011. I am Leah Baum's mother. She is one of your half siblings. Neither of us ever had any contact with you. Yet every time I think of you, I sob. You were not alone. You have brothers and sisters from Maryland to California and from New York to Florida. Like you, all of your donor siblings have suffered and will suffer. They would have understood your pain as well as your joy. Like you, all of your donor siblings have Moms, and in Leah's case, a Dad, who loves them. I know that I am not the only other parent who has worried that my child, your sister, would kill herself. I can't imagine feeling anything less than my life being over should Leah ever kill herself. How could you not know of your mother's deep and enduring love for you, of the never-ending pain this has caused her? Most people who survive a suicide attempt say they couldn't think of another way for the pain to stop. Suicide is a final act which can never be undone. There are other ways.

Please don't hear this as blame. I know that you did what you thought was best. When I have felt suicidal I have been in so much pain that I couldn't imagine ever feeling better. I was wrong. Thoughts and feelings are just thoughts and feelings. Everything in life changes. Sometimes things get better; sometimes they get worse. As long as we are alive there is hope.

I don't know how to tell Leah that you killed yourself. She will never get to meet you either. I know that she will wish like many others, that if she had known you, maybe she could have helped you to not make that one final decision. I hope that she will finally understand that bipolar disorder and depression can be lethal disorders.

Today I saw your picture for the first time. What a beautiful young woman you were. I love looking at your smile.

I know that you loved your Mom. I have come to love her too. She is doing all that she can to survive and find meaning in your death. I promise you that I will do all that I can to support her in this effort.

May You Rest in Peace.

Love, Wendy Baum

Although the world is very full of suffering, it is also full of the overcoming of it.

~Helen Keller

Dear Mallory,

The Letter That Came Just a Little Too Late

To my little sister Mallory;
I never met you,
But in my heart, I've known you.
You are my sister,
As Kate likes to say,
My sister from the same mister.

The sisters; Leah, Mallory, Sarah, Kate,
Another Sarah, Olivia, Alexis, and also Dinah
I'm sure there are more
Plus the brothers too--
This was our crew.
But now we are one less, without you.

Depression can turn into a tragic kill.
They say there's something wrong with us,
"So here take this pill"

Mallory; we all struggle, we all feel pain
We all hurt, we're all slightly insane.
We'll tell ourselves whatever--
'But it's just me; it's the way I am.'

We'll say we are fine
Even if we hurt all the time
But we are really F.I.N.E. –
F*@ked-up, Insecure, Neurotic and Emotional

Mallory when the emotional toll fell upon you...
When it was too much for you to bear,
The emotional toll fell upon us all

Everyone who knew you
Everyone who loved you
Everyone who knew the ones who loved you
Everyone who would have loved to have known you--
The emotional toll overflowed onto us all

If I had known you,
And I knew you were in so much pain,
I'd tell you, "You are not alone--
In our crew, in life, we all feel pain"

And if you were like me
You might have asked someone as I did--
"What do you do when you feel pain?"
"What do you do when you are sad?"

A friend I asked,
She said, "Just do this:
Say to yourself ,
'THIS TOO SHALL PASS.'"

Whatever pain you felt that last day...
I wish I could have altered your fate.
Maybe if you had seen this letter,
The letter that came just a little too late

But the message lives on
And your spirit lives on.
So I'll say it again and again
And I will always pass it along:

When you're feeling sad
When you've lost your way
When you hurt so bad
Think to yourself and say
"THIS TOO SHALL PASS"
"THIS TOO SHALL PASS"

Mallory Mallory Mallory...
You're mother lost a part of herself when she lost you.
I'm reaching out to your mother
Giving her back a piece of you
And a piece of you to me

Mallory, your heart and soul will always live on
(I can only imagine)
In that of all the sisters.
The twinkle in your eyes
The twinkle in all our eyes
And your cheeks,
My cheeks, Kate's cheeks....
Yeah... when I met the donor, my first thought was:
YOU! These cheeks come from you!!

My mother would always tell me
Leah, when you lose, don't lose the lesson.
I wish you had learned the lesson, Mallory,
That shared pain, is pain lessened.

We have all lost you,
But we will all never forget the lesson.
We will spread it, we will share it
And make sure that those who are hurting
Are well aware of it

Mallory, I wish you would have shared your pain.
You may have felt different, to many,
But to your crew, to your sisters, we're all the same.
We have lost you,
But we will all never forget the lesson.
We will spread it, we will share it
And make sure that those who are hurting
Are forever informed, and well aware of it

Where there's a will, there's a way,
Shared pain is pain lessened.
We lost you, but we are spreading the lesson.

Depression is real, and can be dangerous.
Treatment is crucial, serious, and imperative.

When you hurt so bad inside
That you want to scream, are about to cry--
When it hurts so bad, that you think you could die--
Think to yourself and say:
"THIS TOO SHALL PASS,
This too shall pass."
I wish you had made it through that day.

RIP Mallory Richards
Much Love and Respect,

The leader of the crew,
Leah Baum, Big sis #1.

Epilogue

When my daughter entered intensive treatment for her depression in 2007, I wrote the following poem, framed it and sent it to her in Utah as a reminder not only of my deep love for her, but of my abiding conviction in her ability to overcome whatever challenges might come her way. Four years later, its' words of love and encouragement hung helplessly on Mallory's bedroom wall just several feet from where she would end her life.

Magnificently loving to all who know her
Youthful exuberance, the world has been her oyster

Daring and brave, has abundant courage
Angel to the animals, she wants to change the world
Underdogs enjoy her compassion
Giddy about acting
Helpful and kind
Teaches me every day what's important and what's not
Every day I love her more
Respect, ambition and intelligence are strengths of hers

Makes me forever grateful that I am her mother
Actually makes me laugh more than anyone I know
Learns and teaches something valuable every day
Lean on me more, Mally, and I will be there for you
Observe the love you give, then give it to yourself
Run toward your dreams, be unstoppable in this
You are powerful and priceless. Now believe that.

Whoever you are, and whatever your reasons for reading this book, thank you. It's not one of those fun, fluffy things to read, with a happy ending.

But it *is* a love story as much as it is a wake-up call. For us all.

You and I have work to do.

And it begins with ourselves.

Observe the love you give, then give it to yourself.
Run towards your dreams, be unstoppable in this.
You are powerful and priceless. Now believe that.

~~Lisa Richards

Appendix A

Statistics

In 2009, there were 36,909 suicides reported in the United States. [1]

Every 14.2 minutes in the United States, someone dies by suicide. [2]

One million people attempt suicide yearly in the United States alone. [3]

Approximately 1,100 college students in the United States kill themselves every year. [4]

Roughly 100,000 teenagers worldwide kill themselves every year. [5]

It is estimated that one million people worldwide kill themselves each year. That translates to approximately one suicide every forty seconds. It is predicted that by 2020, a suicide will occur somewhere in the world every twenty seconds. [6]

2,3,4   Centers for Disease Control and Prevention

5, 6   World Health Organization

Appendix B

HOTLINES AND RESOURCES FOR PEOPLE IN CRISIS

National Hopeline Network
www.hopeline.com
1-800-442-HOPE (4673)

National Suicide Prevention Hotline
1-800-273-TALK (8255)

 Didi Hirsch Los Angeles Suicide Prevention Crisis Line
1-877-7-CRISIS or 1-877-727-4747

Befrienders Worldwide
www.befrienders.org
(For International Hotlines)

Suicide and Crisis Hotlines
www.suicidehotlines.com
1-310-895-2326

Spanish Speaking Suicide Hotline
1-800-SUICIDA (784-2432)

Grad Resources and National Graduate Student Hotline
www.gradresources.org
1-800-GRADHLP (472-3457)

Postpartum Support International
www.postpartum.net (for women with perinatal depression or anxiety)
1-800-944-4773, 1-800-944-4PPD

Online Journaling and "venting" website
The Suicide Project
www.suicideproject.org

FOR TEENS

TeenScreen
www.teenscreen.org
1-212-265-4453

Teen Line
www.teenlineonline.org
1-800-852-8336

Teen Suicide
www.teensuicide.us

The Jason Foundation
www.jasonfoundation.com
1-615-264-2323

Trevor Line (LGBTQ)
www.thetrevorproject.org
866-488-7386

YouthLine
www.youthline.us
1-877-YOUTHLINE (968-8454)

Active Minds – Mental Health Awareness Programs for College Students
www.activeminds.org
1-202-332-9595

RESOURCES FOR INDIVIDUALS WHO HAVE LOST LOVED ONES

Friends for Survival, Inc.
www.friendsforsurvival.org
1-916-392-0664

Heartbeat – Grief and Support Following Suicide
www.heartbeatsurvivoraftersuicide.org

Survivors After Suicide Support Groups
www.survivorsofsuicide.com
1-310-895-2326

Compassionate Friends (for parents who have lost children)
www.compassionatefriends.org
1-310-368-6645 (in Los Angeles County)
1-630-990-0010

Survivors Road2Healing
www.road2healing.com

Before Their Time
www.beforetheirtime.org

Crisis, Grief and Healing
www.webhealing.com

Greifnet
www.griefnet.org
Parents of Suicide/Friends and Families of Suicides
www.pos-ffos.com

Sibling Survivors
www.siblingsurvivors.com

The Suicide Memorial Wall
www.suicidememorialwall.com

Alliance of Hope for Suicide Survivors
www.allianceofhope.org
1-847-8683313

FOR VETERANS

Vet2Vet
www.veteranscall.us
1-877-VET2VET (838-2838)

Veteran Crisis Hotline
1-800-273-8255

Suicide Wall
www.suicidewall.com

EDUCATIONAL RESOURCES ON SUICIDE

AFSP- American Foundation for Suicide Prevention
www.afsp.org
1-888-333-2377

AAS – America Association of Suicidology
www.suicidology.org
1-202-237-2280

National Institute of Mental Health
www.nih.gov/health/topics/suicide-prevention

NOPCAS – National Organization for People of Color Against Suicide
www.nopcas.com
1-202-549-6039

QPR Institute – Question, Persuade and Refer
www.qprinstitute.org
1-888-726-7926

SAVE – Suicide Awareness/Voices of Education
www.save.org
1-952-946-7998

Yellow Ribbon Suicide Prevention Project, Light for Life International
www.yellowribbon.org
1-303-429-3530

Centers for Disease Control and Prevention
www.cdc.gov
1-800-232-4636

Suicide Prevention Resource Center
www.sprc.org
1-877-GET-SPRC (438-7772)

RESOURCES FOR MENTAL ILLNESS

Los Angeles County Department of Mental Health
www.dmh.lacounty.gov
1-800-854-7771

National Alliance on Mental Illness
www.nami.org
800-950-6264
1-916-567-0163 (in California)

Mental Health America
www.nmha.org
1-800-969-6642

New Middle Press
www.newmiddlepress.com
25202 Crenshaw Blvd. #200
Torrance, California 90505
Phone: 866 693-0443
Fax: 310 325-5431

Mail Order Form

Rates Effective June 1, 2012
Subject to change without notice

Dear Mallory: Letters To A Teenage Girl Who Killed Herself

_____$15.00   Paperback ISBN 978-0-9853189-0-1
$3.50 s/h

All profits from the sale of *Dear Mallory* go to helping people at risk for suicide.

Date:_____   Email:_____

Name:_____

Address:_____

City/State/Zip Code:_____

Day Telephone Number:_____

Please include check or money order made out to New Middle Press

**California residents must pay appropriate taxes.